My Soul

as I see it

Volume III

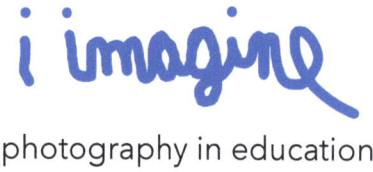

photography in education

i.imagine, Inc.
306 Greenup Street, Covington, KY 41011
www.iimaginephotography.org

Printed in the United States of America
First edition, first printing

Published by: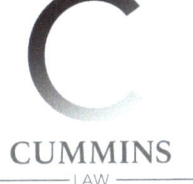

Library of Congress-in-Publication Data

ISBN: 978-0-9993752-1-1

This project was made possible by the following sponsors:

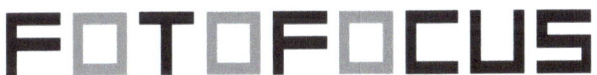

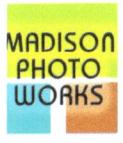

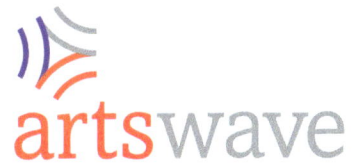

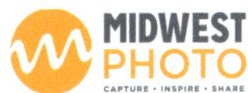

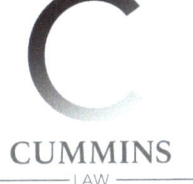

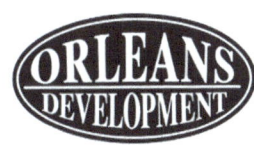

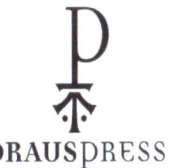

i.imagine's mission is to
educate
empower
inspire
support
connect
engage
people through the lens

Introduction

For most people, the future is a constant hum that influences the decisions you make on a daily basis. Many might agree that the way that you feel about yourself today greatly impacts the way in which you picture yourself in the future. With the future in mind, i.imagine embarked on a journey with twenty amazing students of Holmes Middle School in Covington Kentucky. With a mission to convince them of the beauty that lies within themselves, their families, their school, and their neighborhood, students shared family photos, took a hop on-hop off bus tour of Covington, and participated in regular photos walks on the grounds of their school.

From September of 2017 to May of 2018, i.imagine met with Holmes Middle School students to educate, inspire, and empower them through the lens of a camera. In a positive, judgment free zone, students opened up and shared a glimpse of what beauty looks like through their lens.

In the end, i.imagine was left with an overwhelmingly powerful collection of images that reflect the beauty that surrounds these students every day. Our hope for our incredible young photographers is that they remember that although you may not always have control over things that happen in your future, you do control the the lens in which you choose to look through.

Over 900 images were carefully selected and printed onto four-inch tiles, which were then organized to compose a twelve-foot mural at Ninth Street and Madison Avenue in Covington Kentucky. i.imagine hopes that this mural will serve as an archive and symbol of the beauty of Holmes Middle School, The City of Covington and it's people.

About This Book

The 100 images printed in this book were selected from images displayed on i.imagine's tile mural located at the corner of Ninth Street and Madison Avenue in Covington Kentucky.

Thank you for supporting i.imagine and it's students. With each page, we hope your imagination takes you to great places. Enjoy!

Thank You

FotoFocus and ArtsWave for believing in our big ideas and for supporting the arts and education in Covington. We are more beautiful thanks to you!

Holmes Middle School for always opening your doors with a warm welcome and allowing i.imagine the privilege of working with your amazing students.

Megan Morford of Covington Partners for accommodating our every need. We could not have done this without you!

Madison Photo Works for your continuous support of i.imagine exhibitions which now include 900 or so photo tiles.

Orleans Development for generously sharing your wall with us.

Richard Hunt of Praus Press for saying yes and being an i.imagine champion.

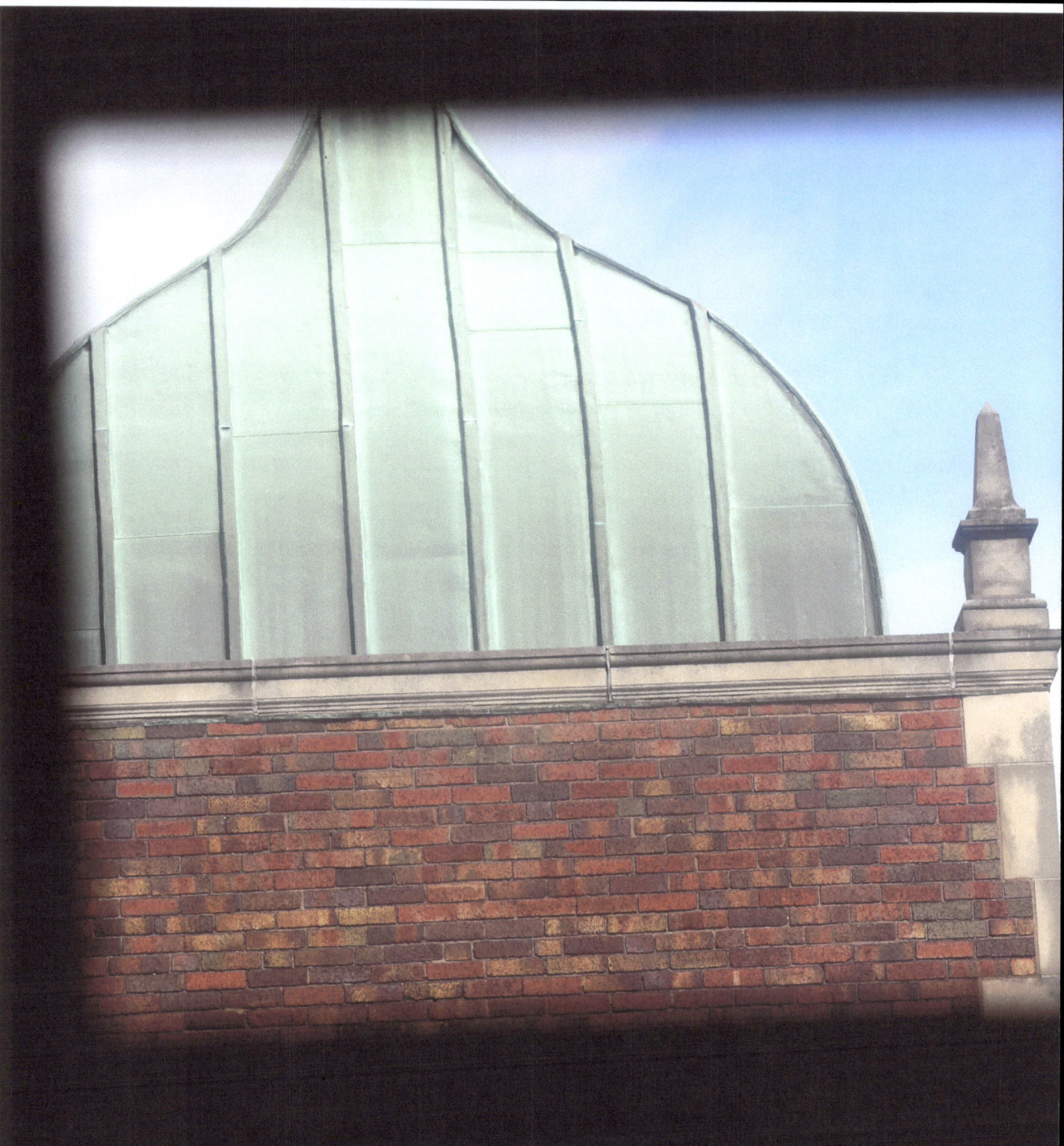

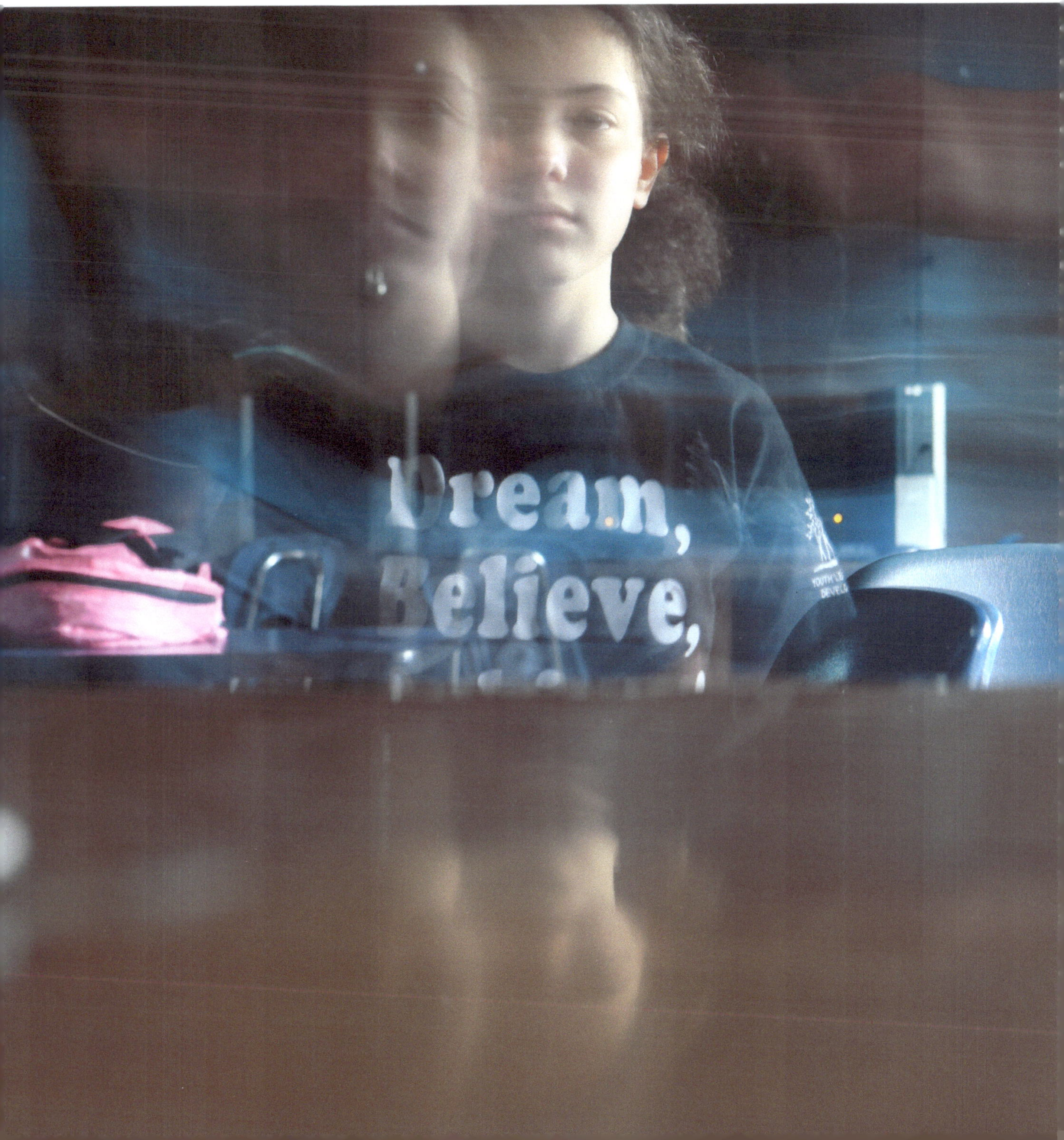

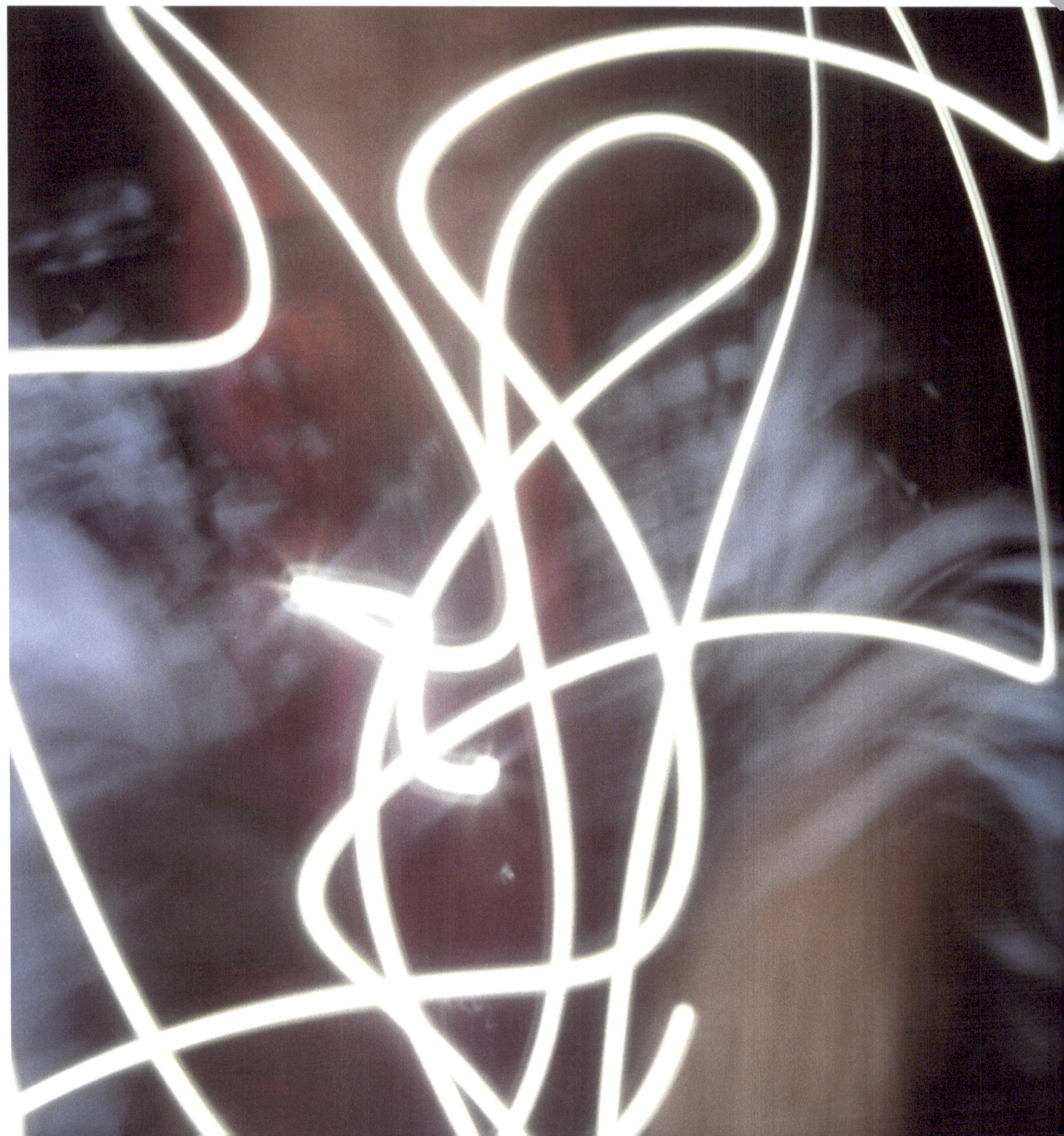

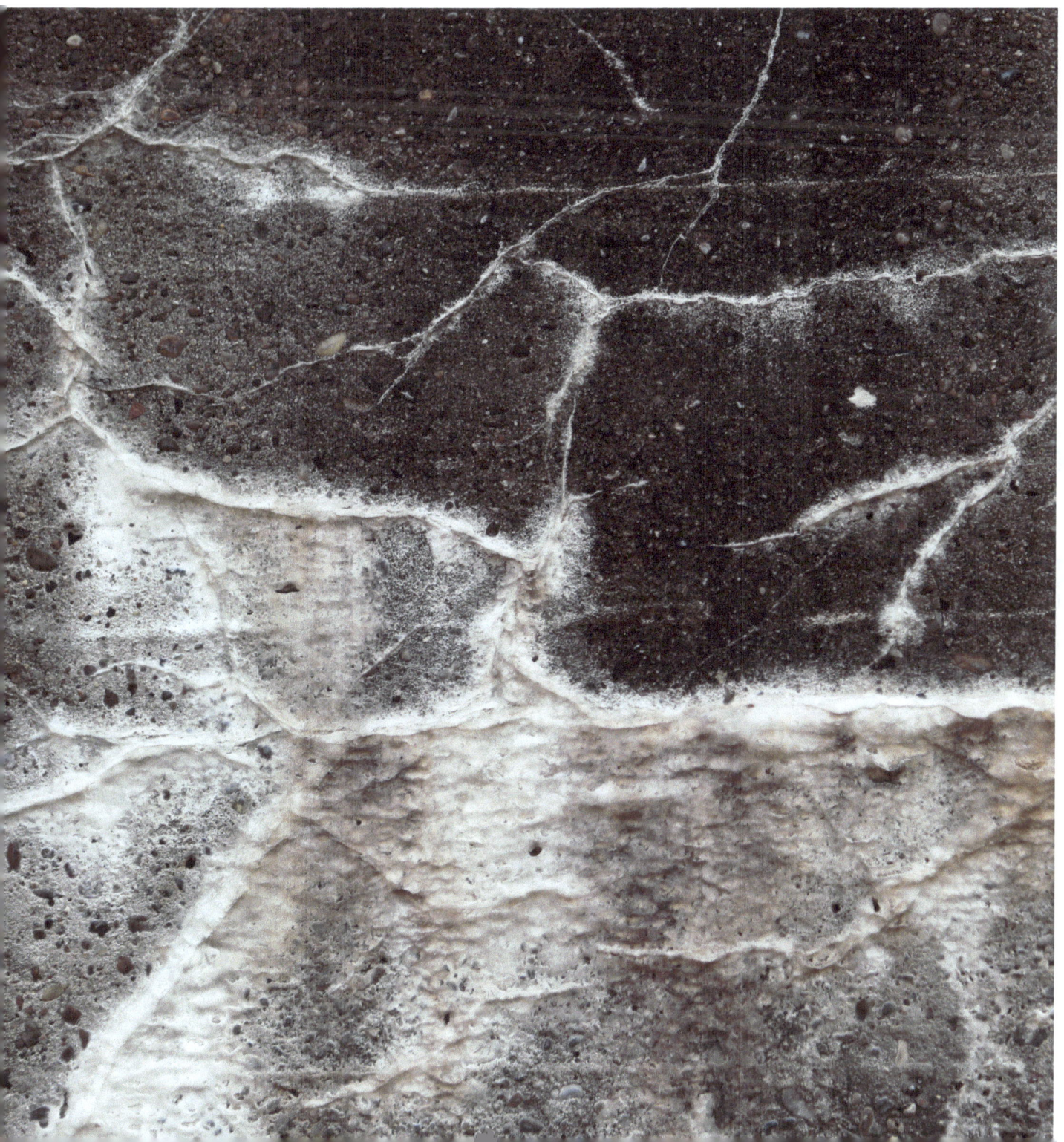

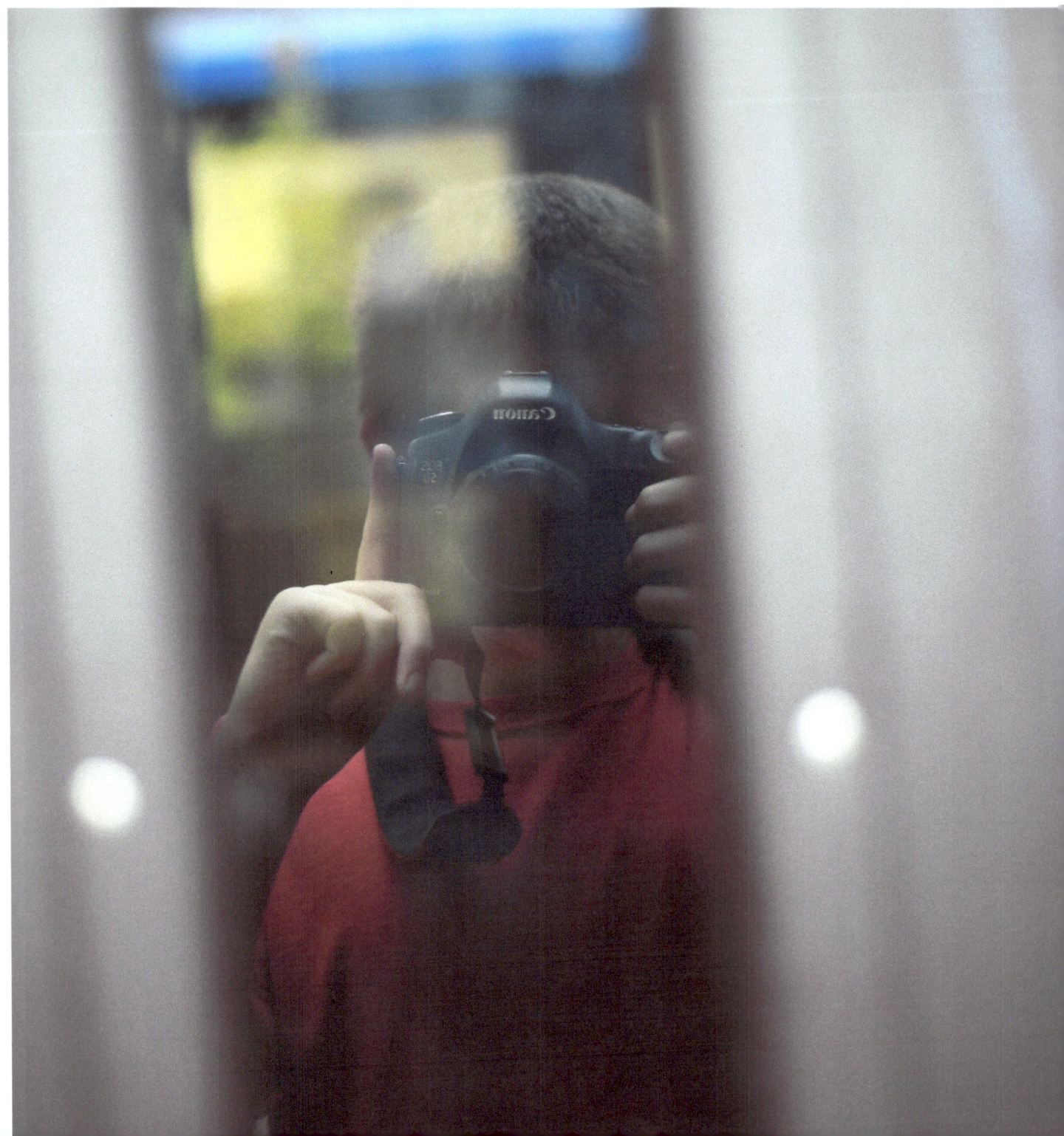

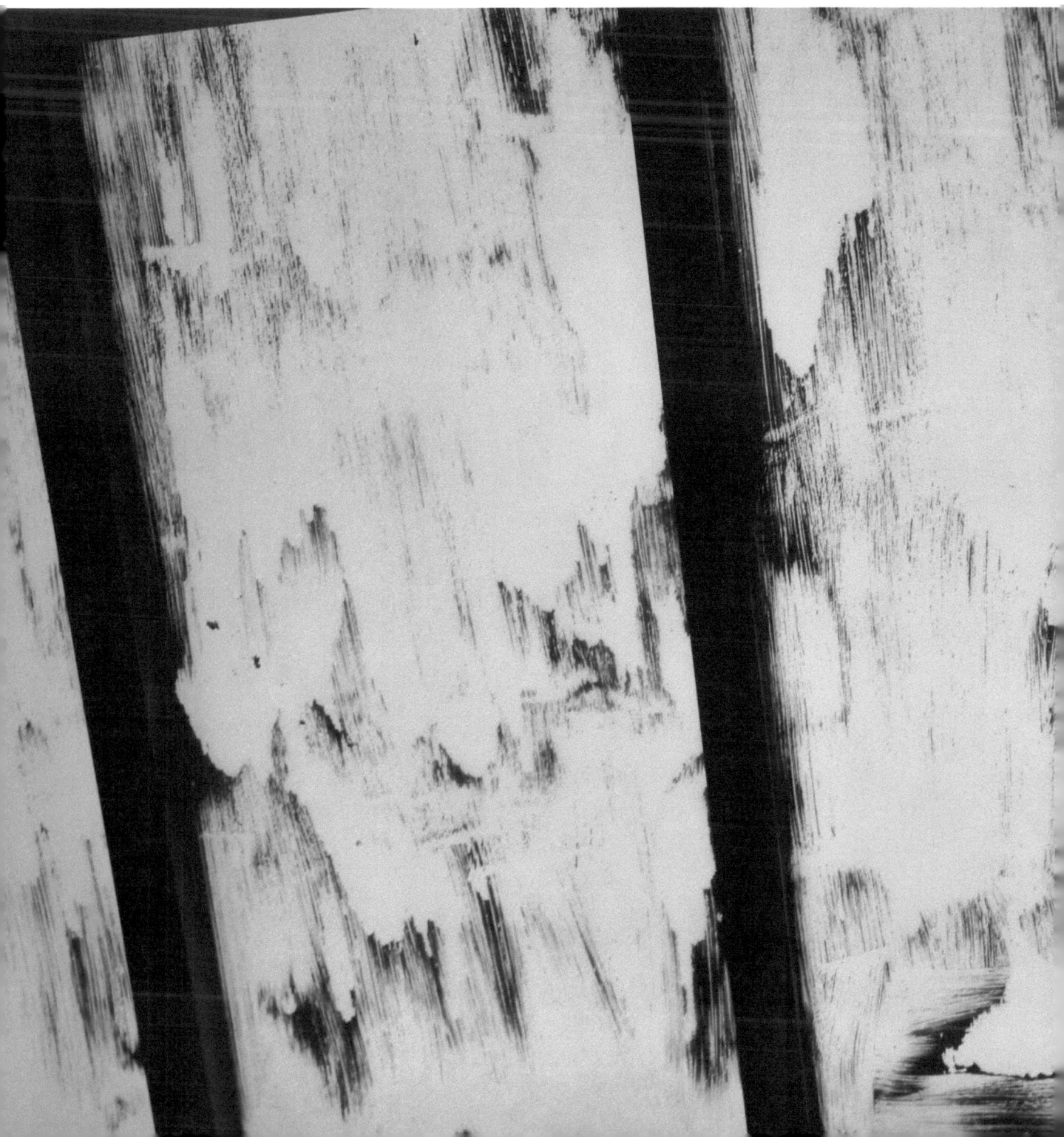

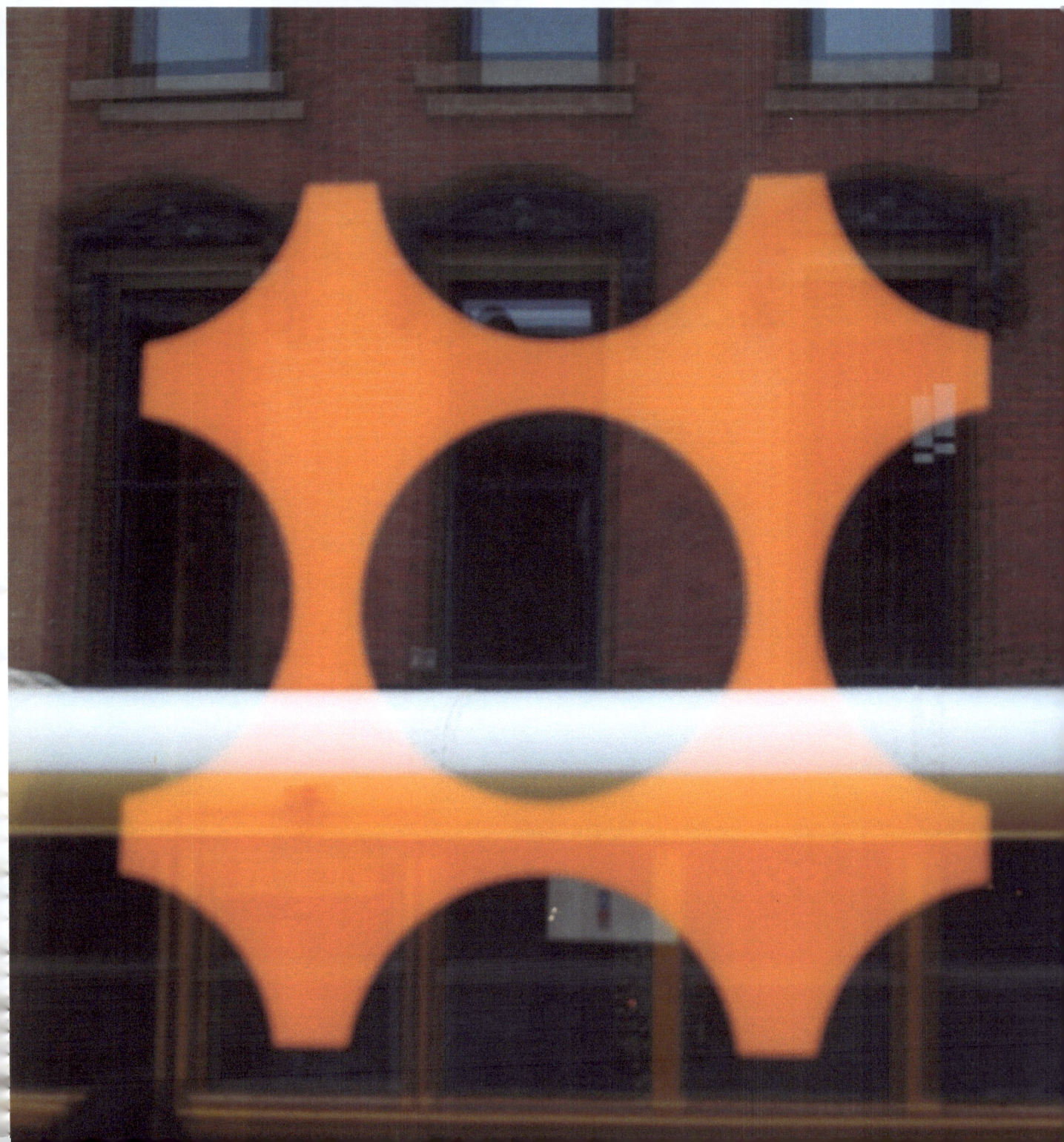

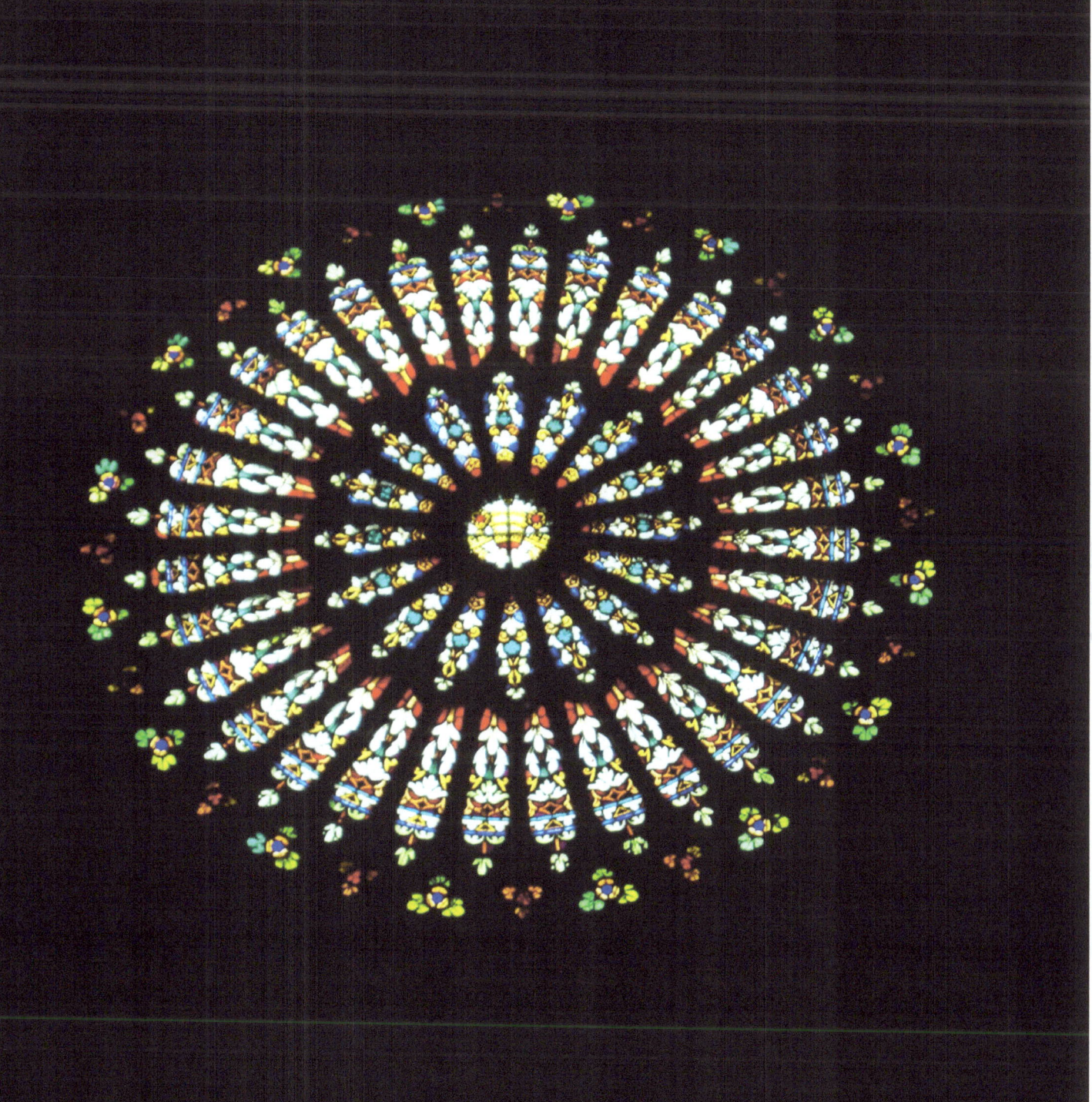

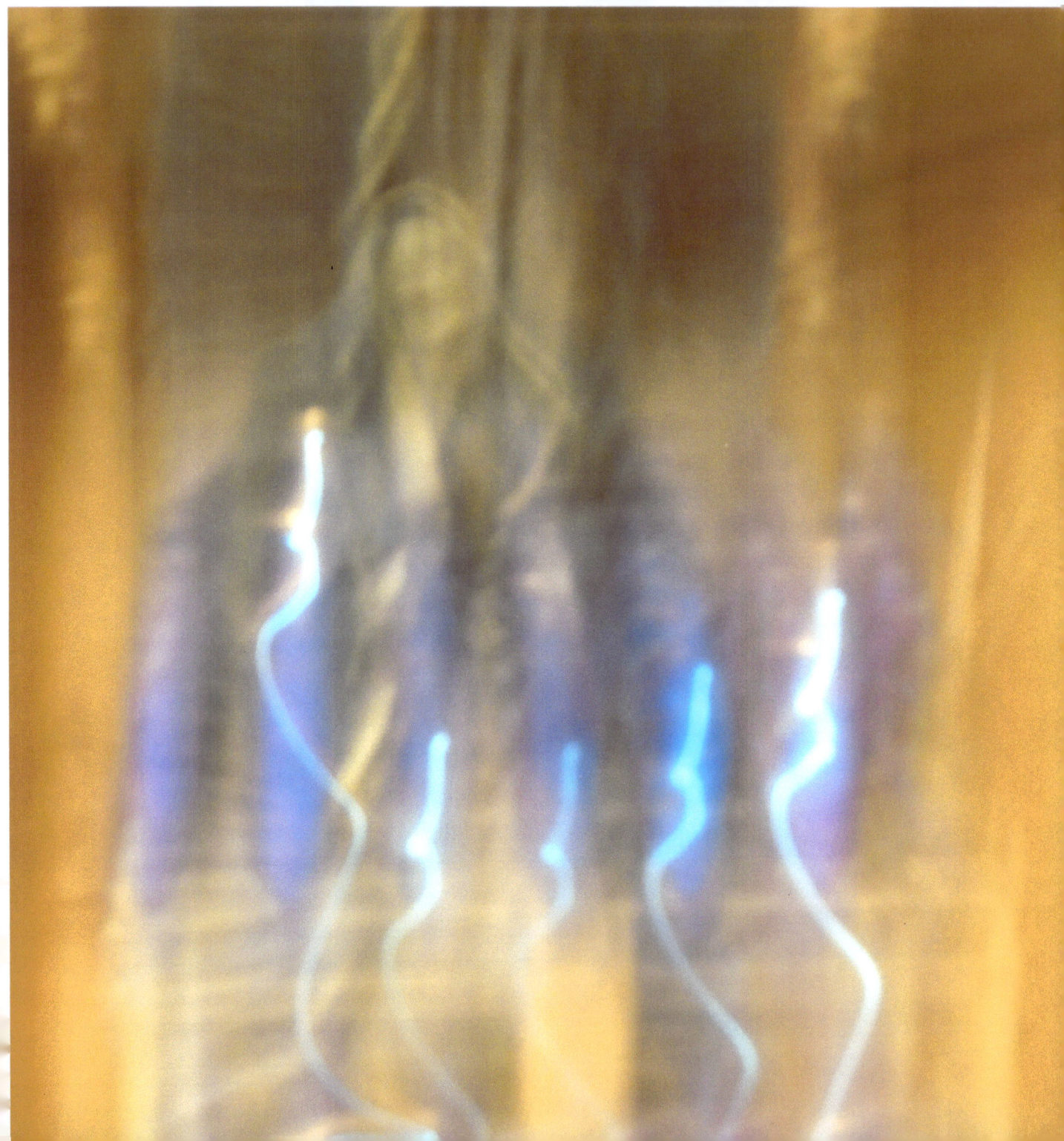

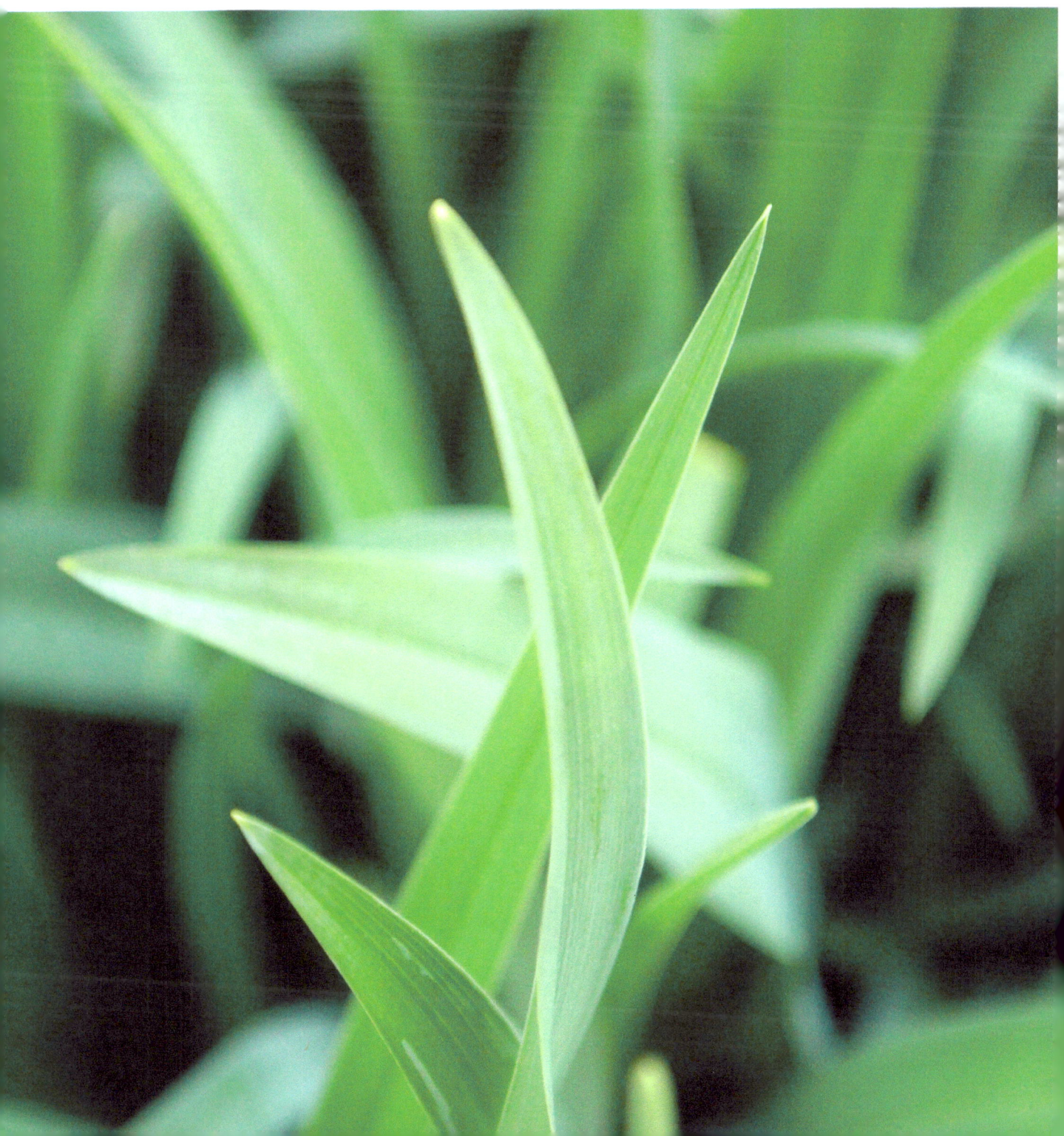

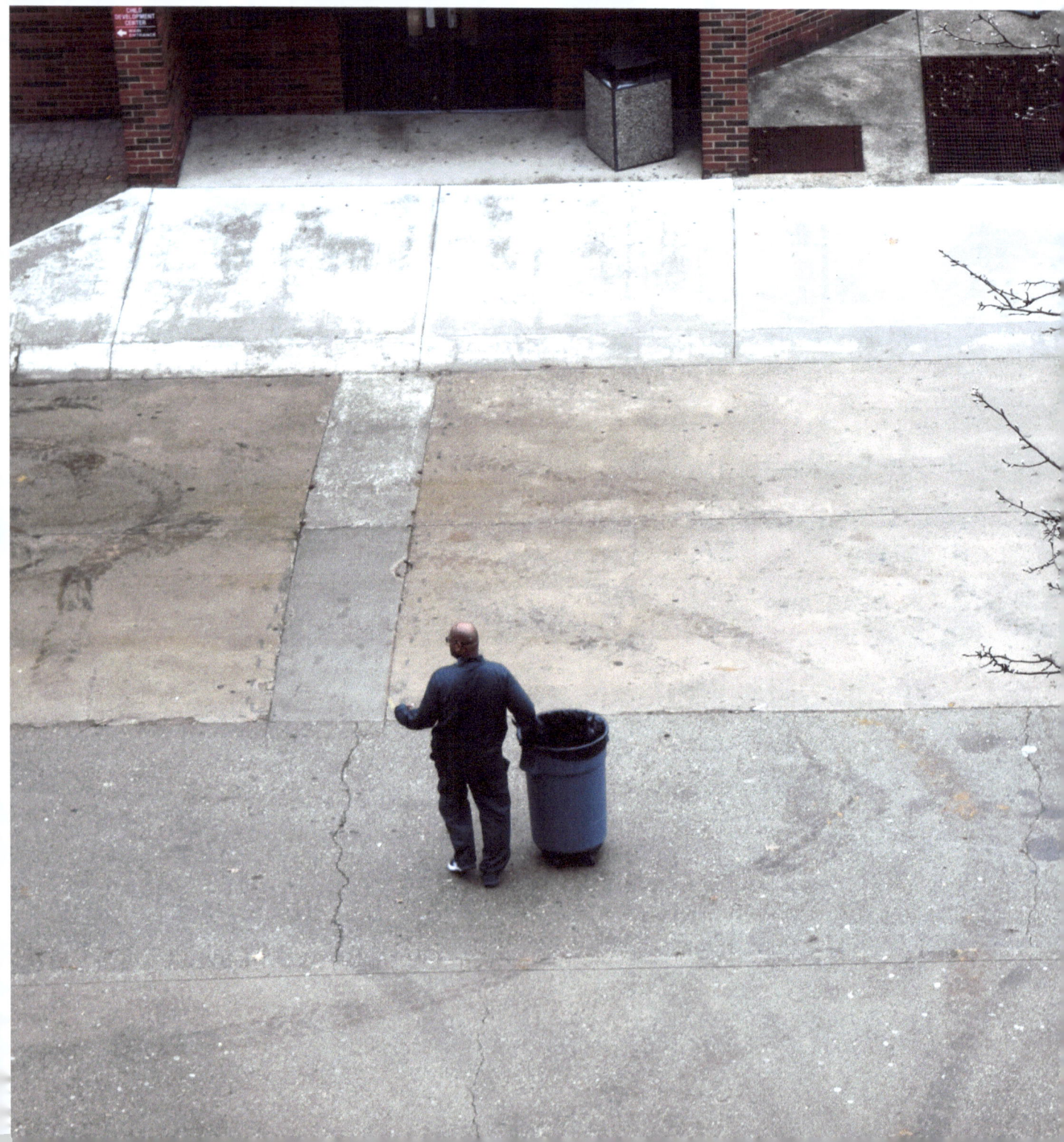

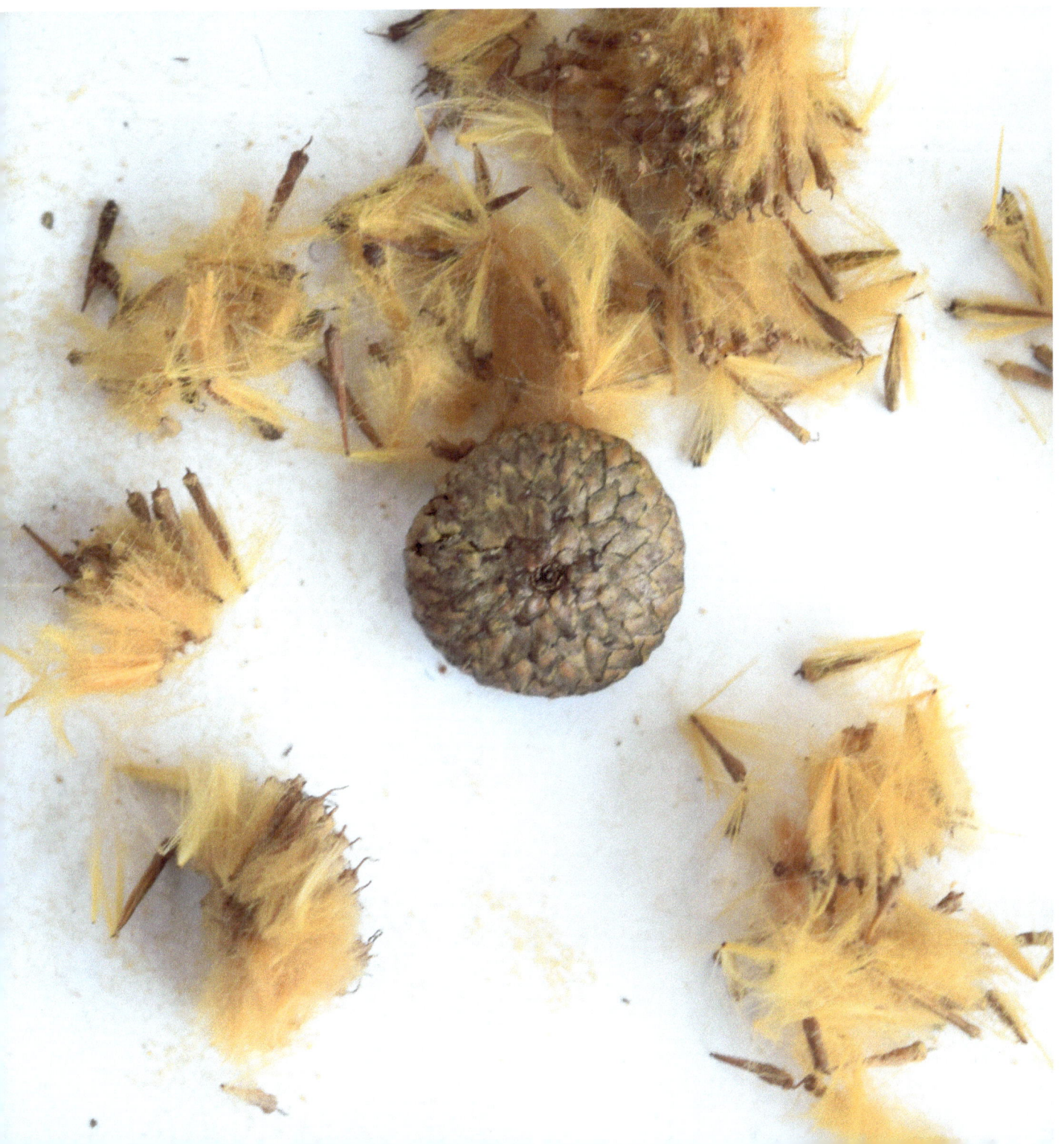

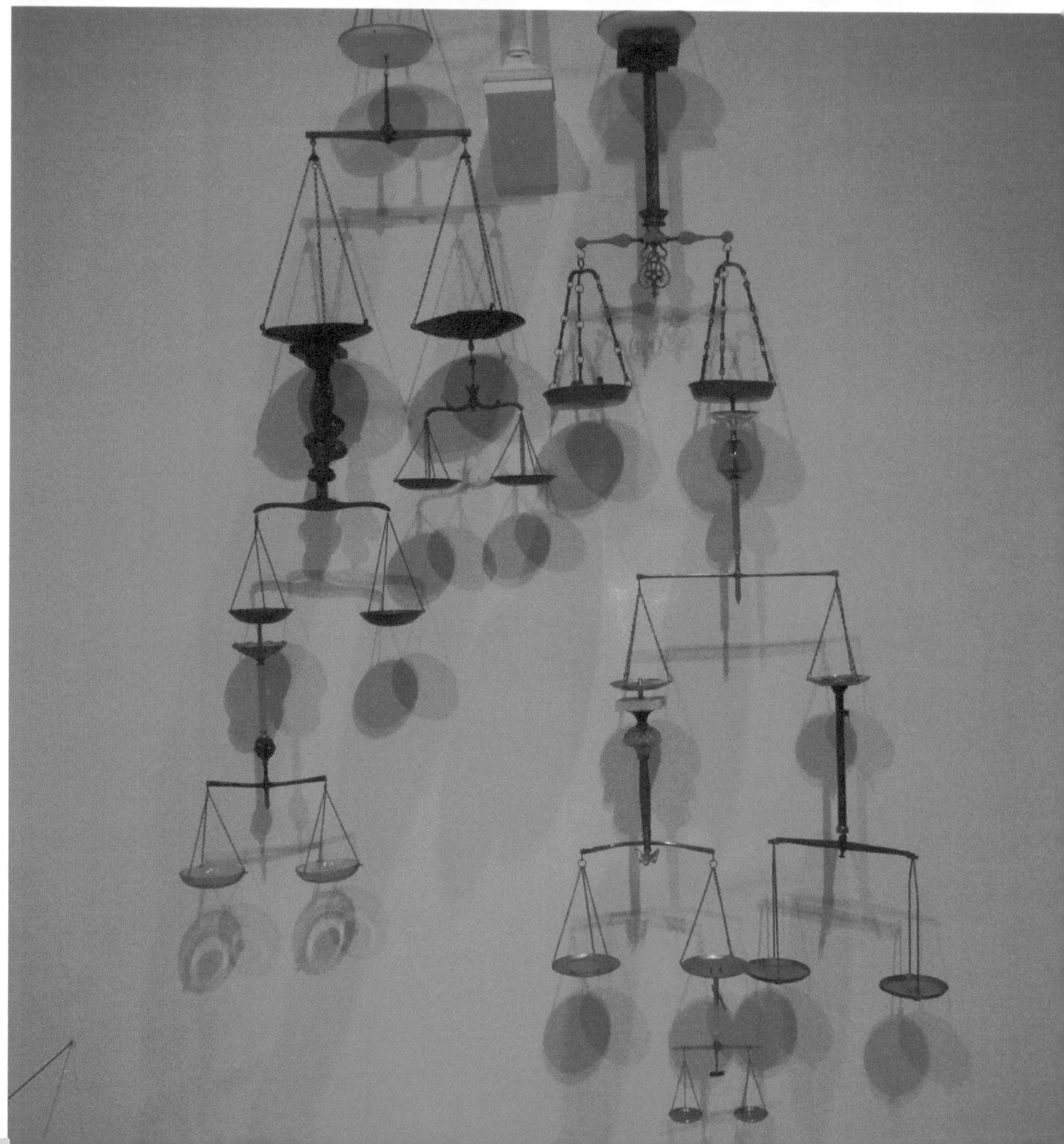

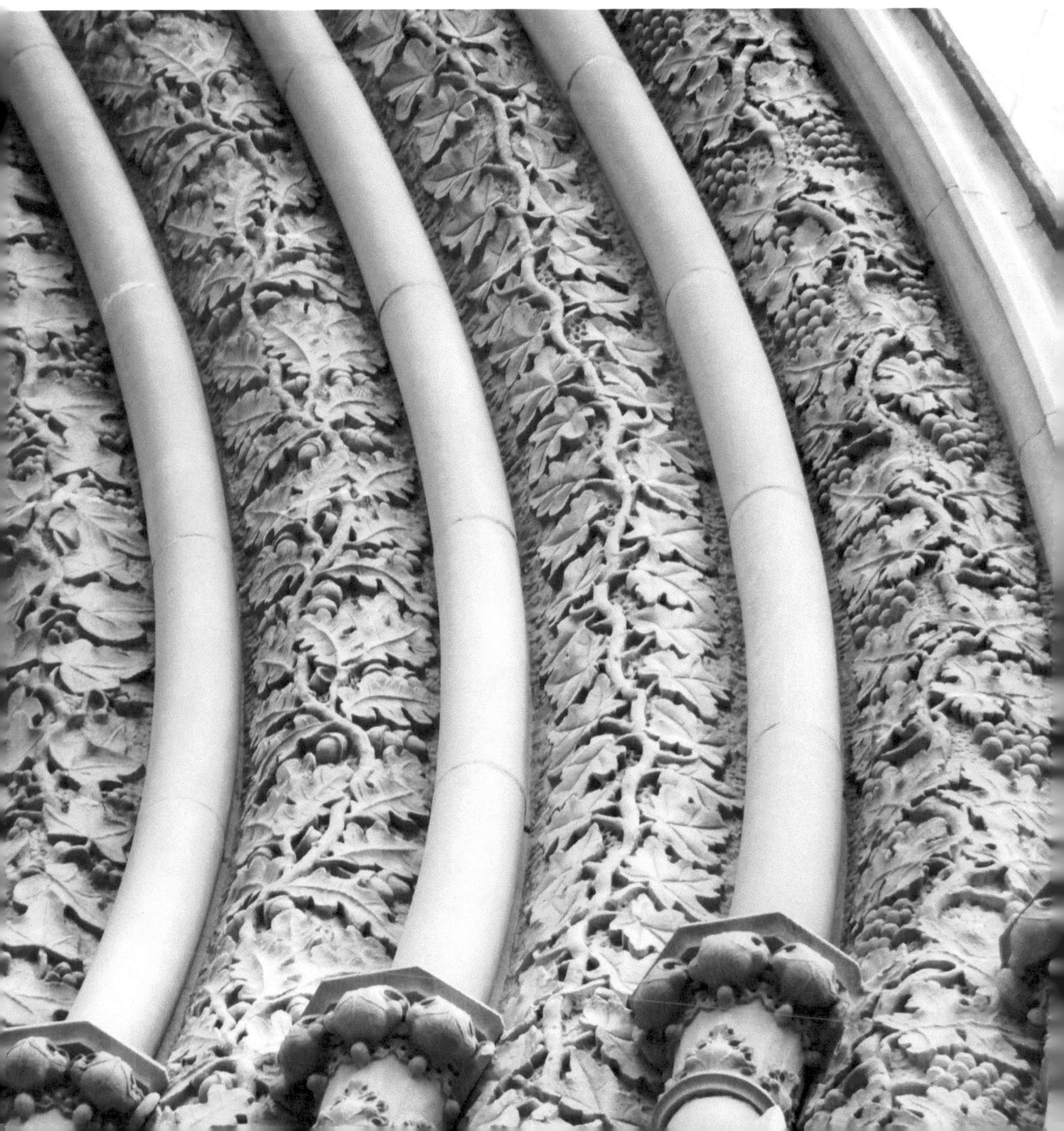

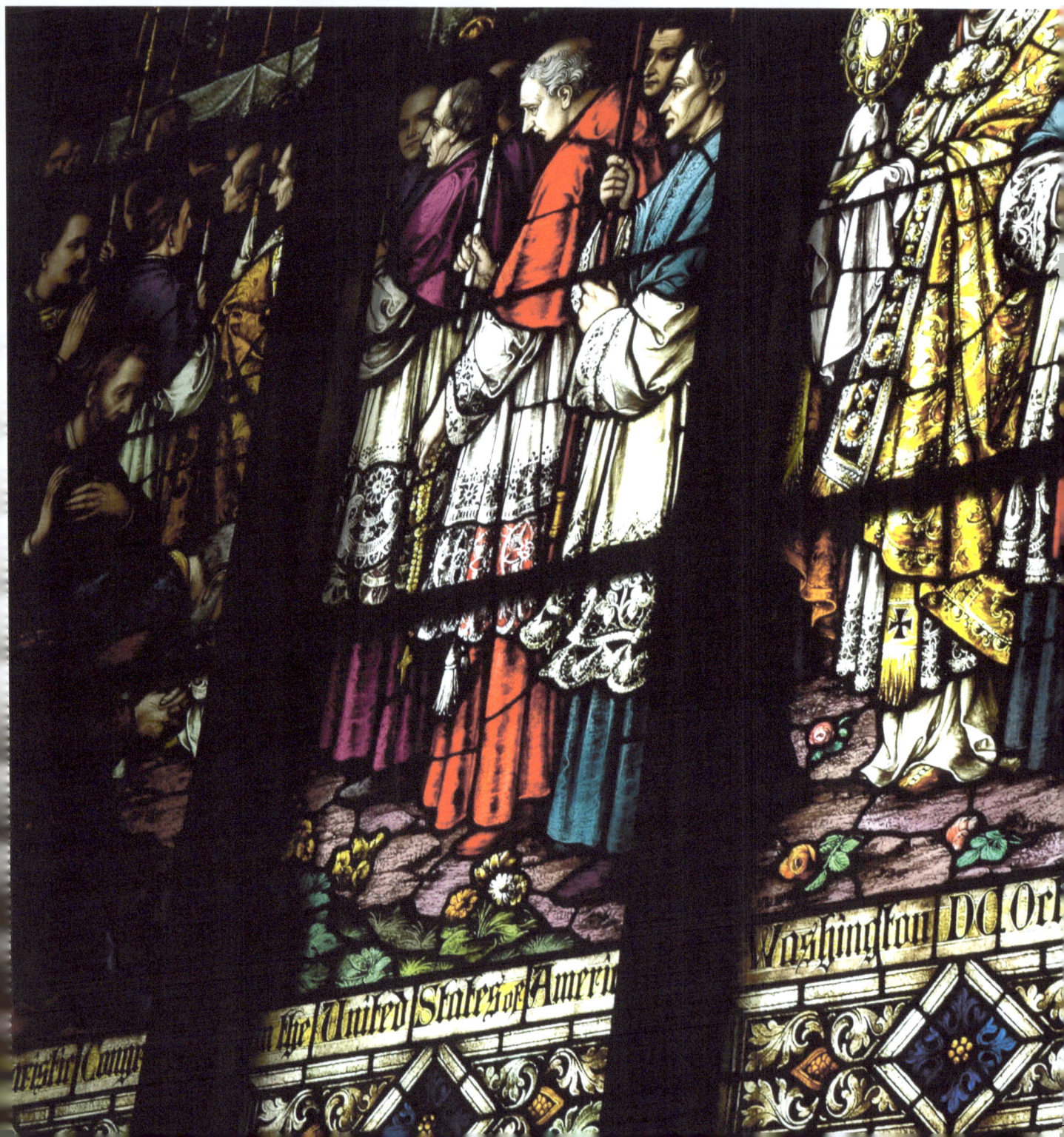

the United States of America

Washington DC Or[...]

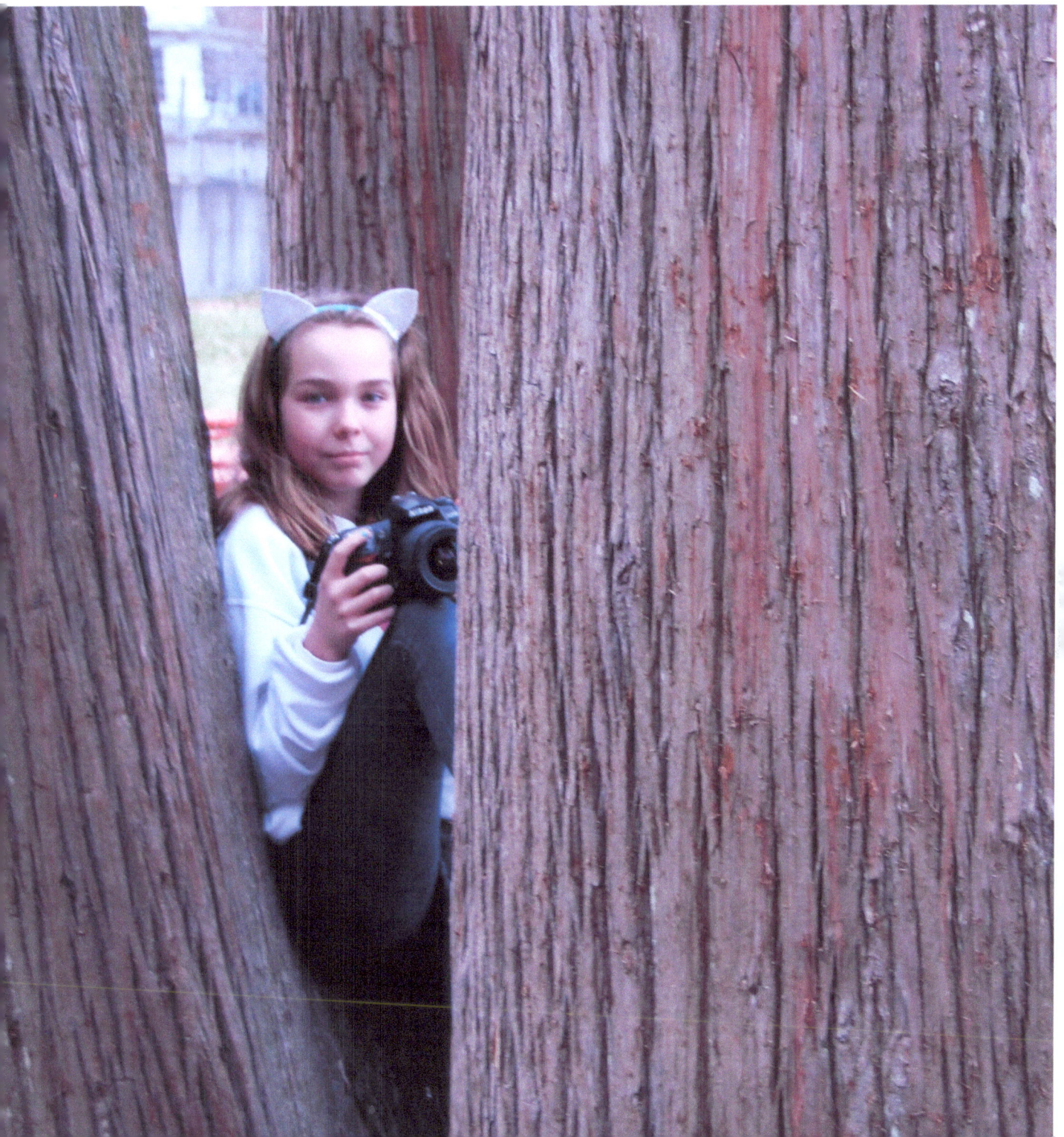

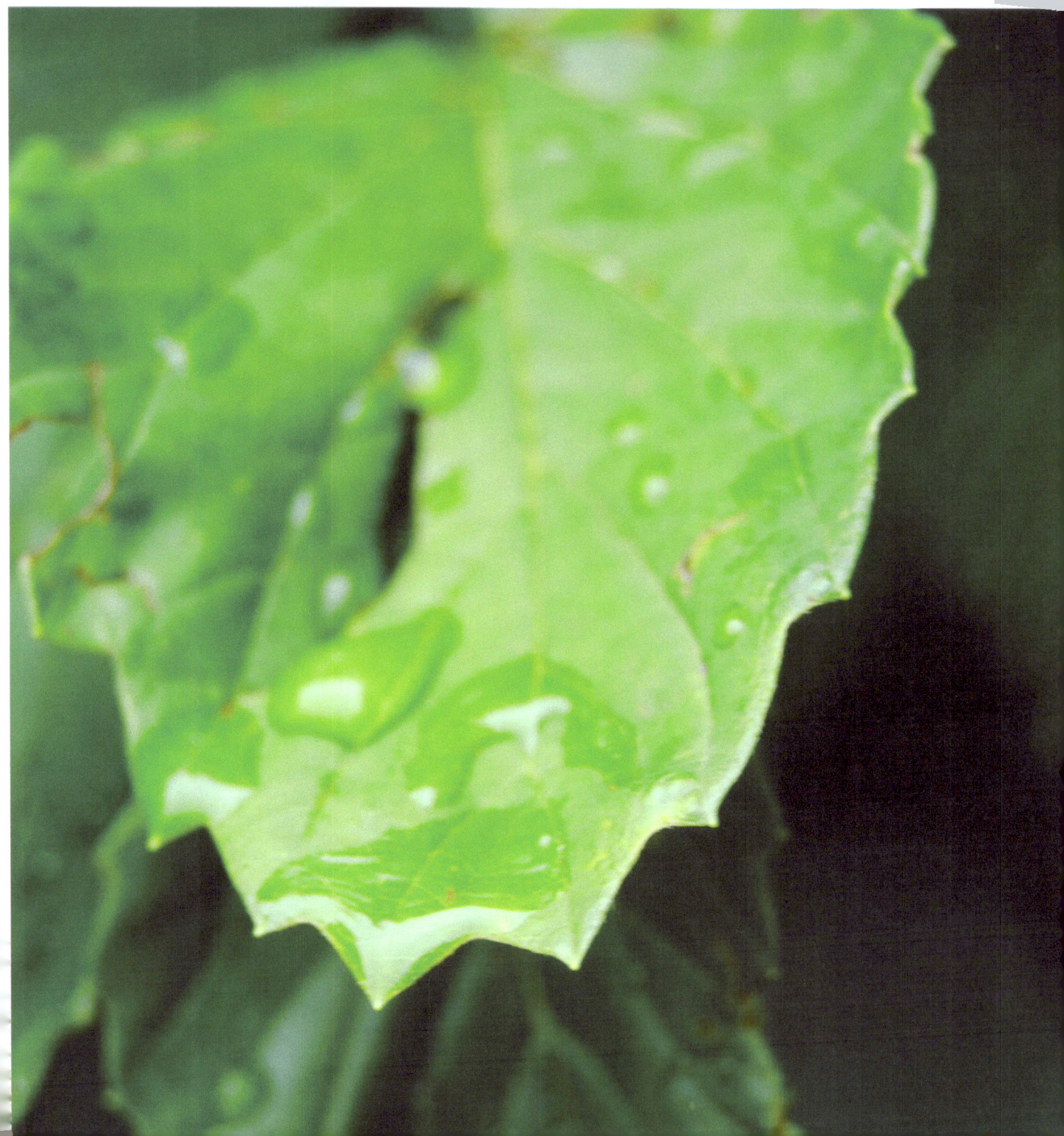

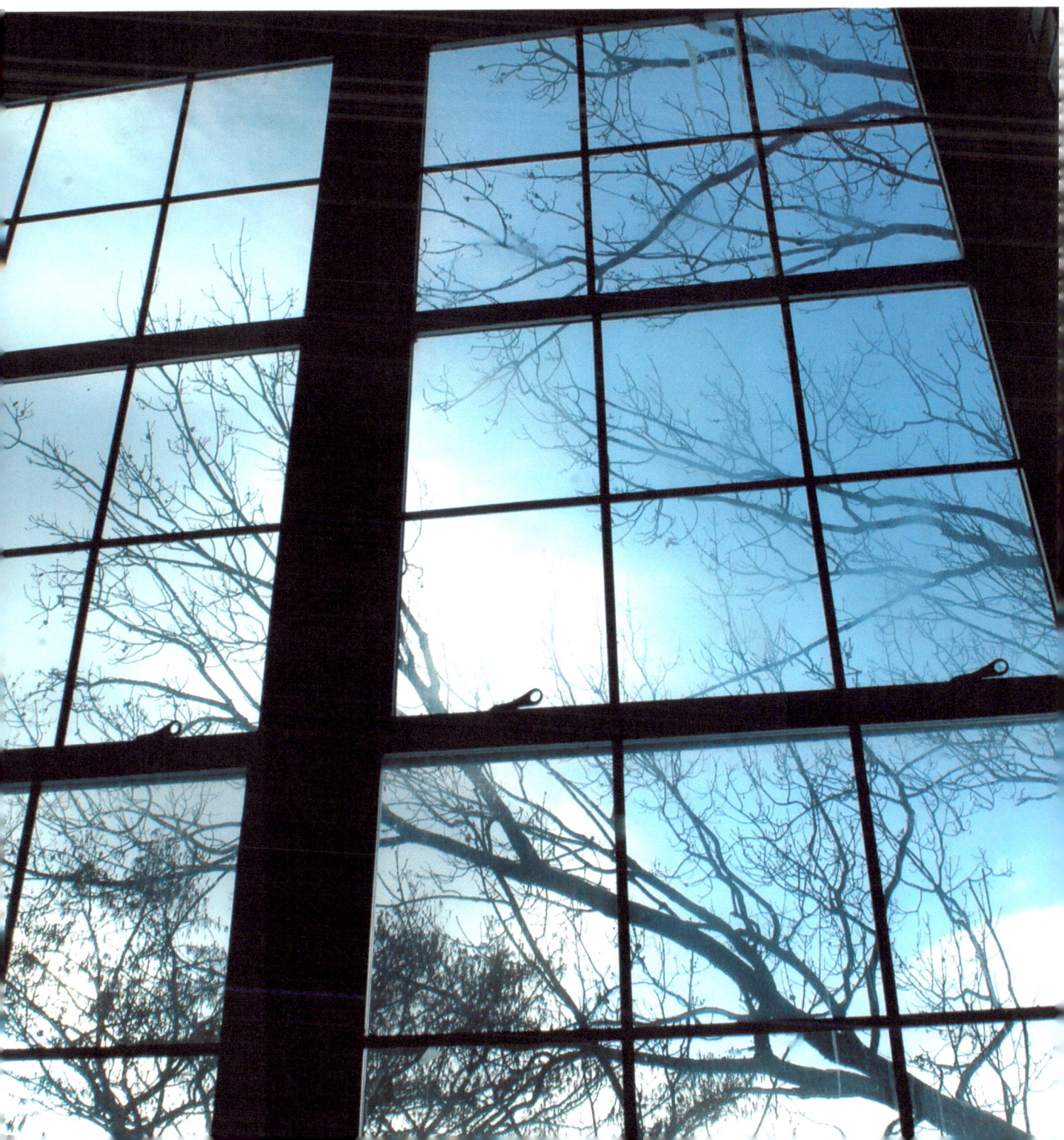

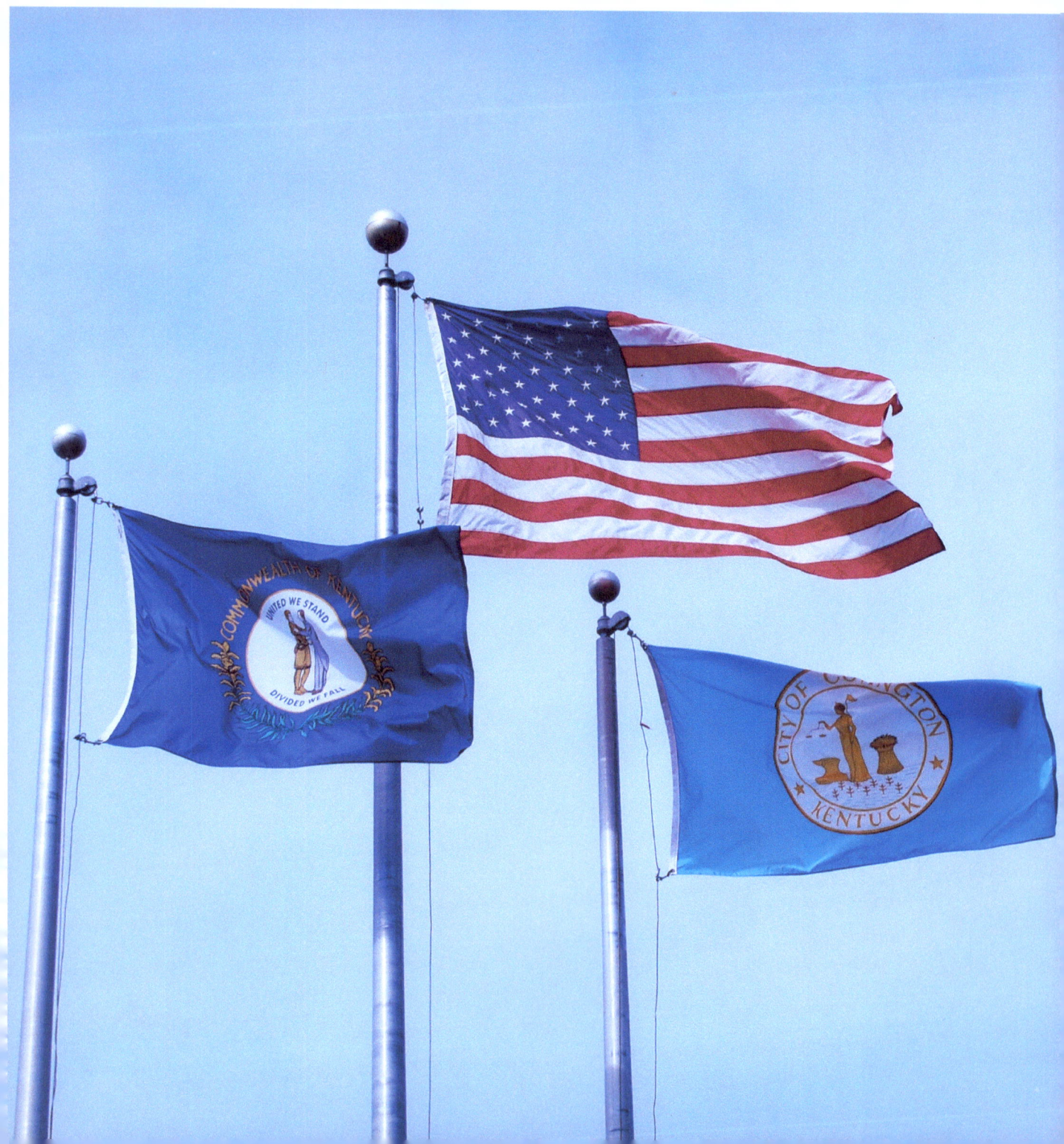

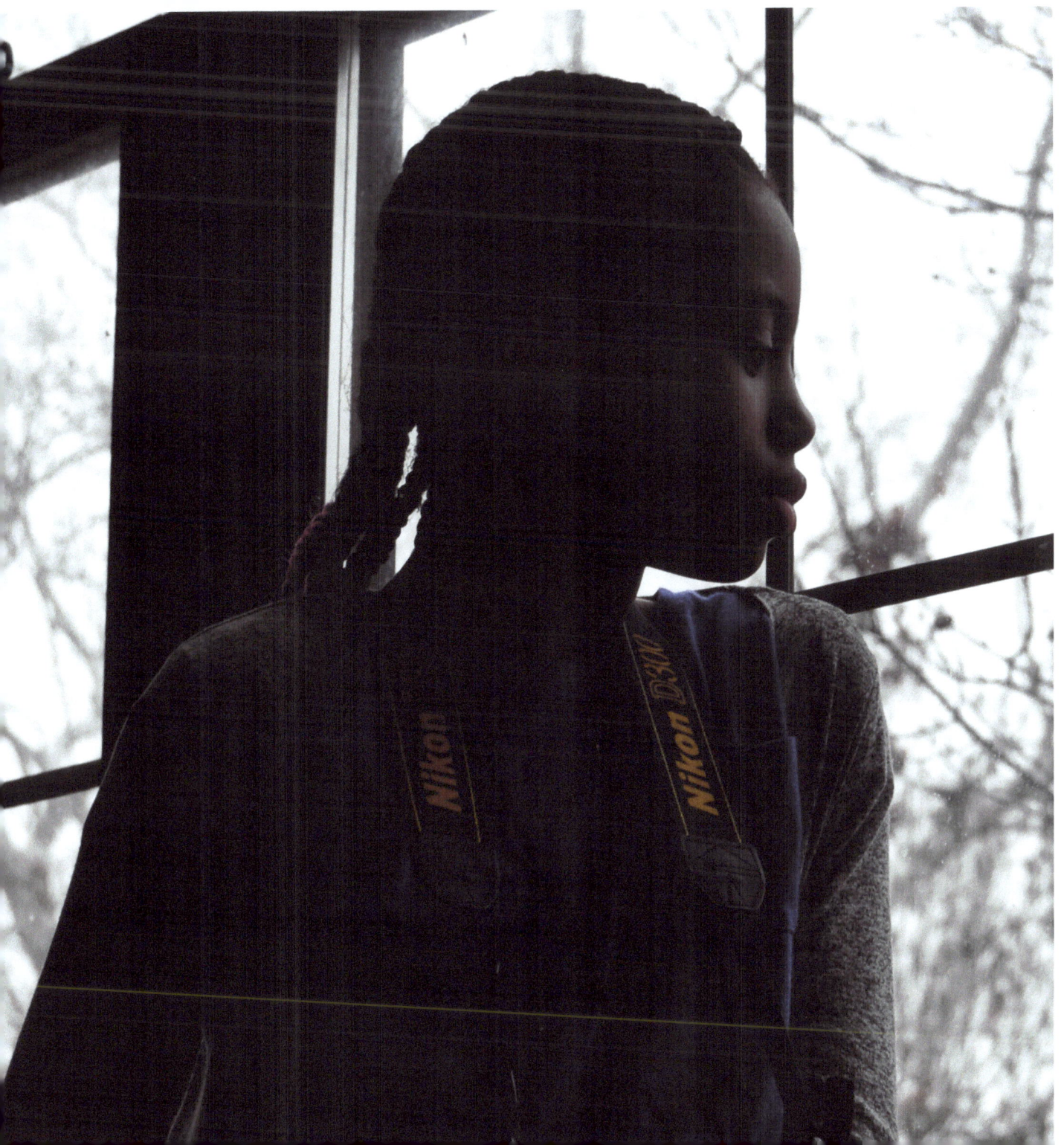

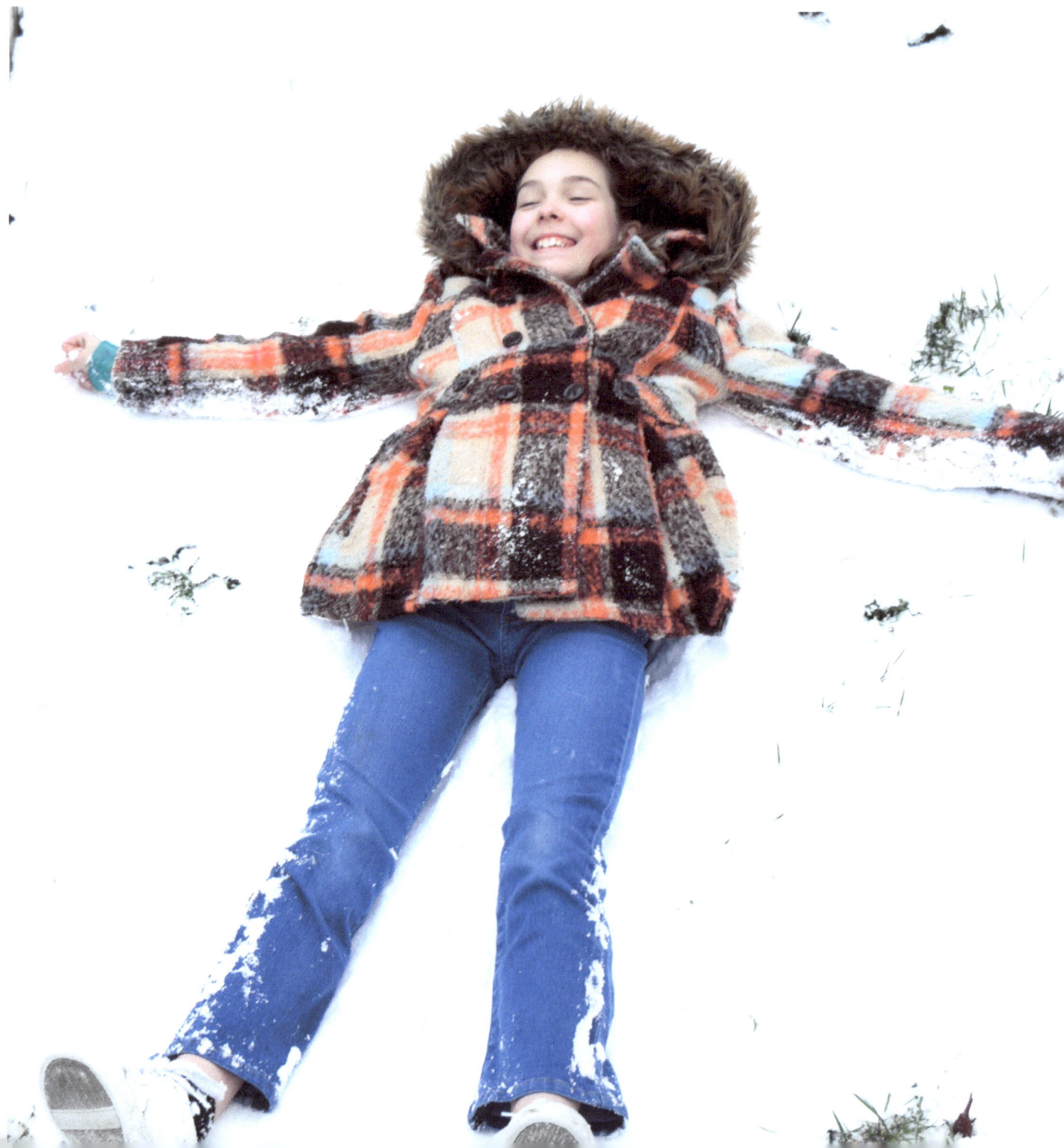

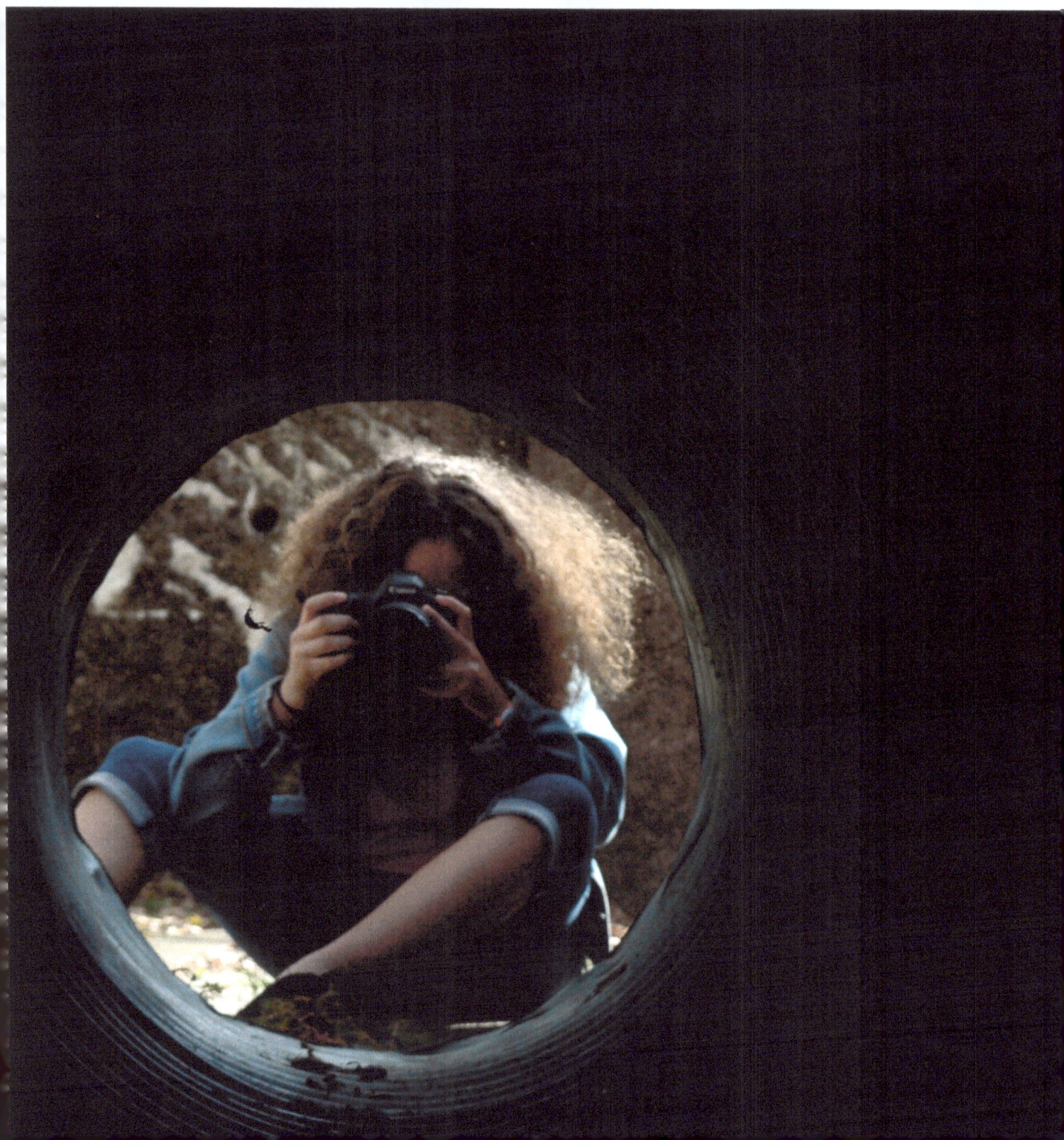

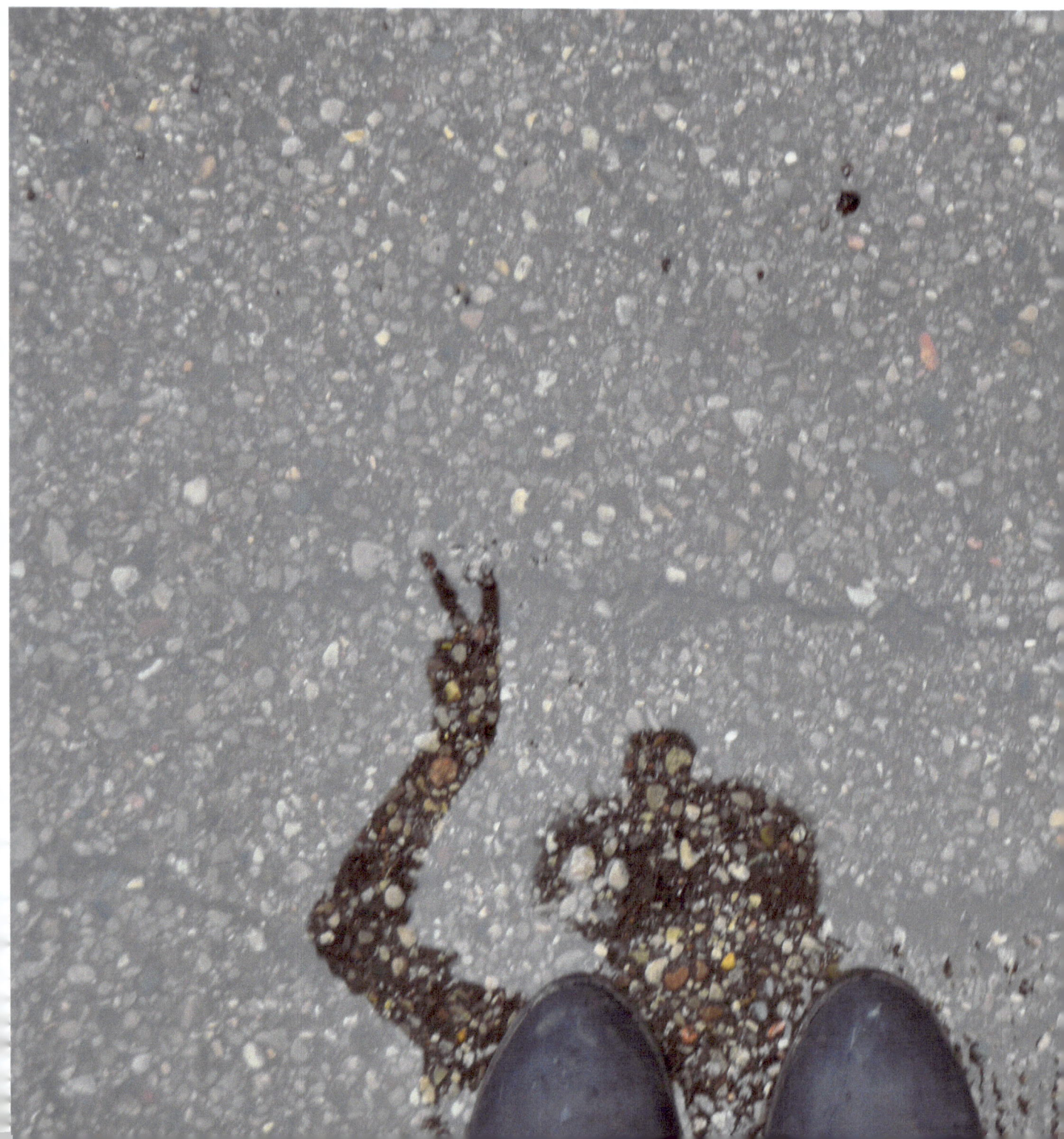

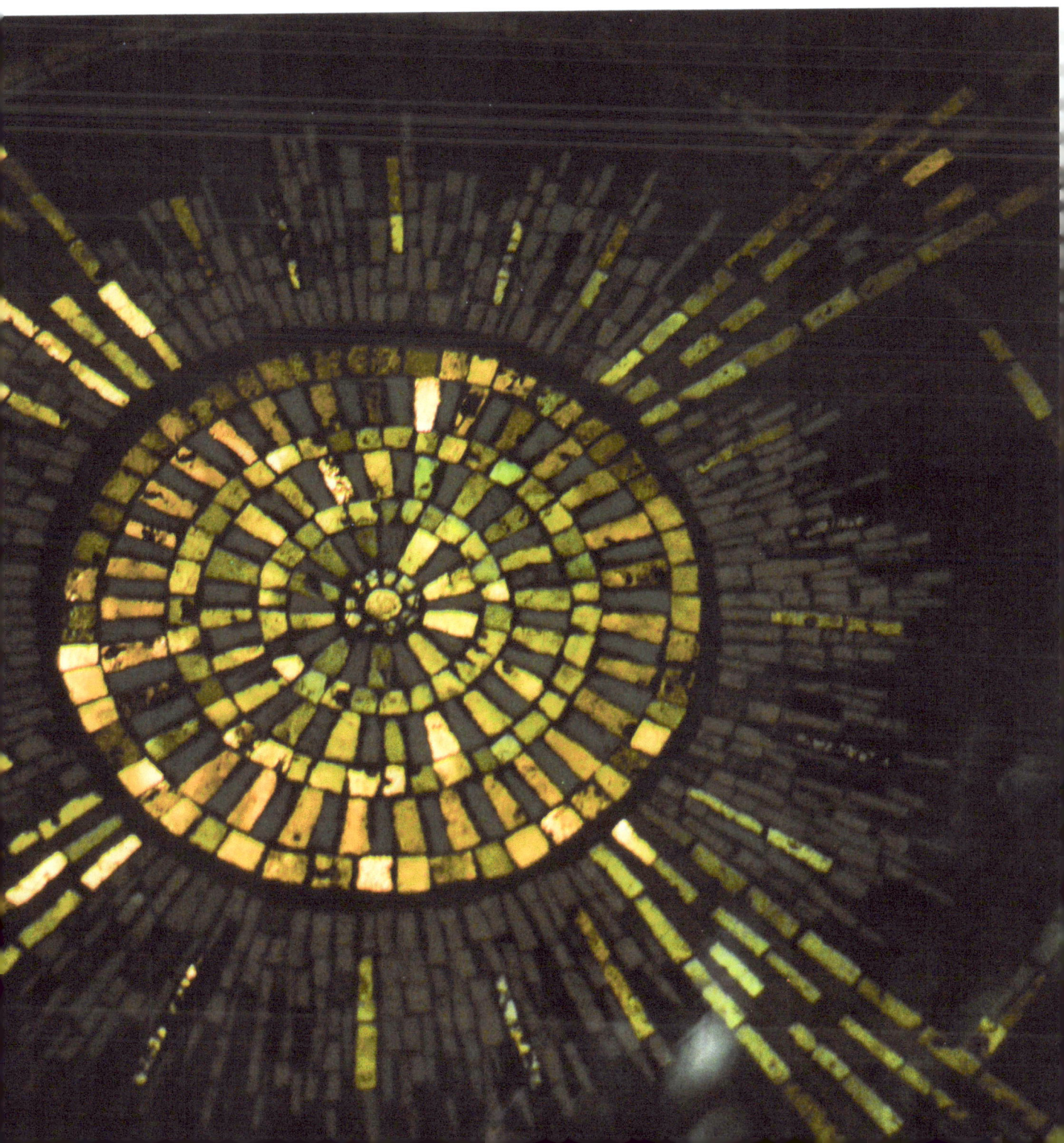

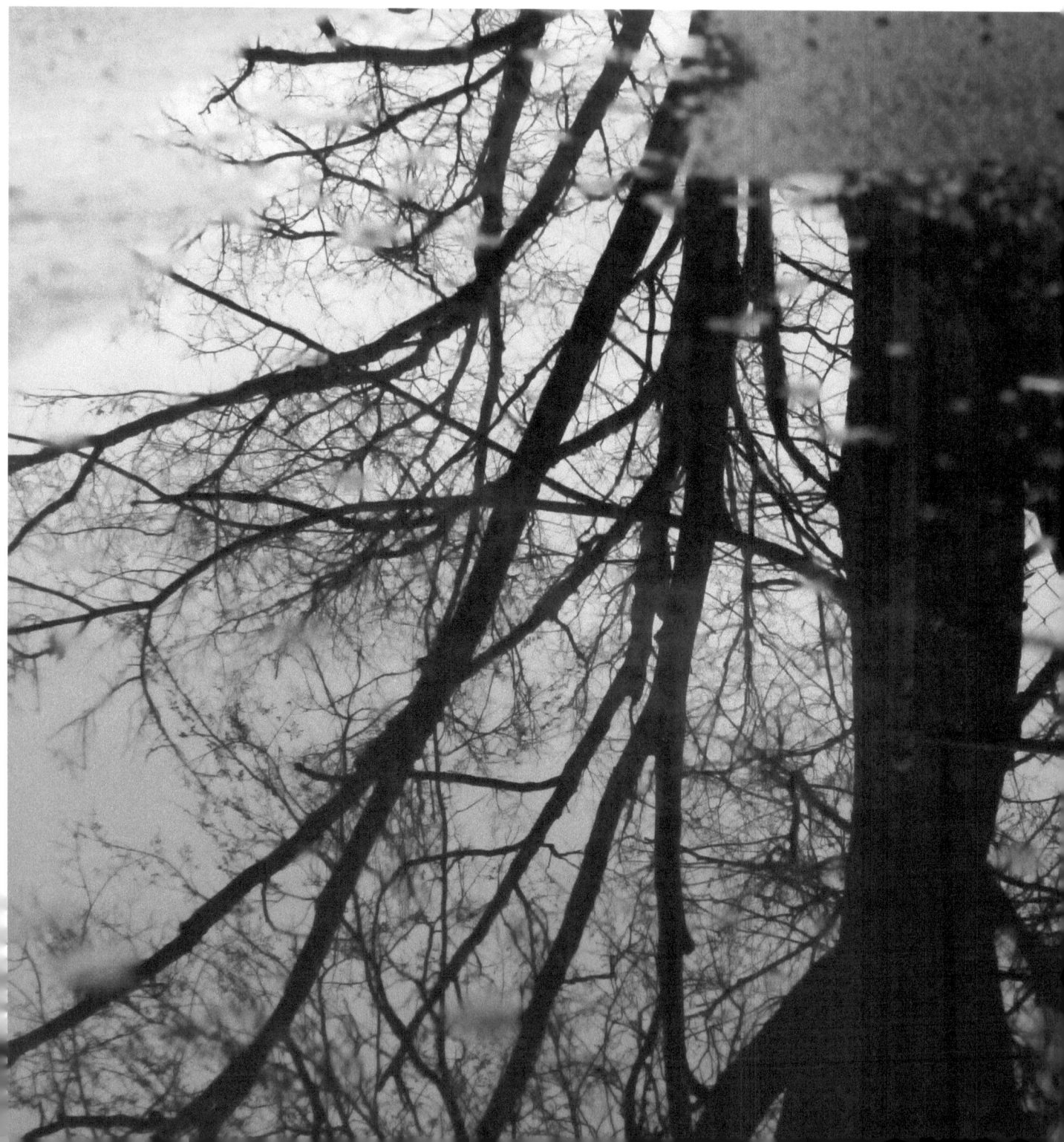

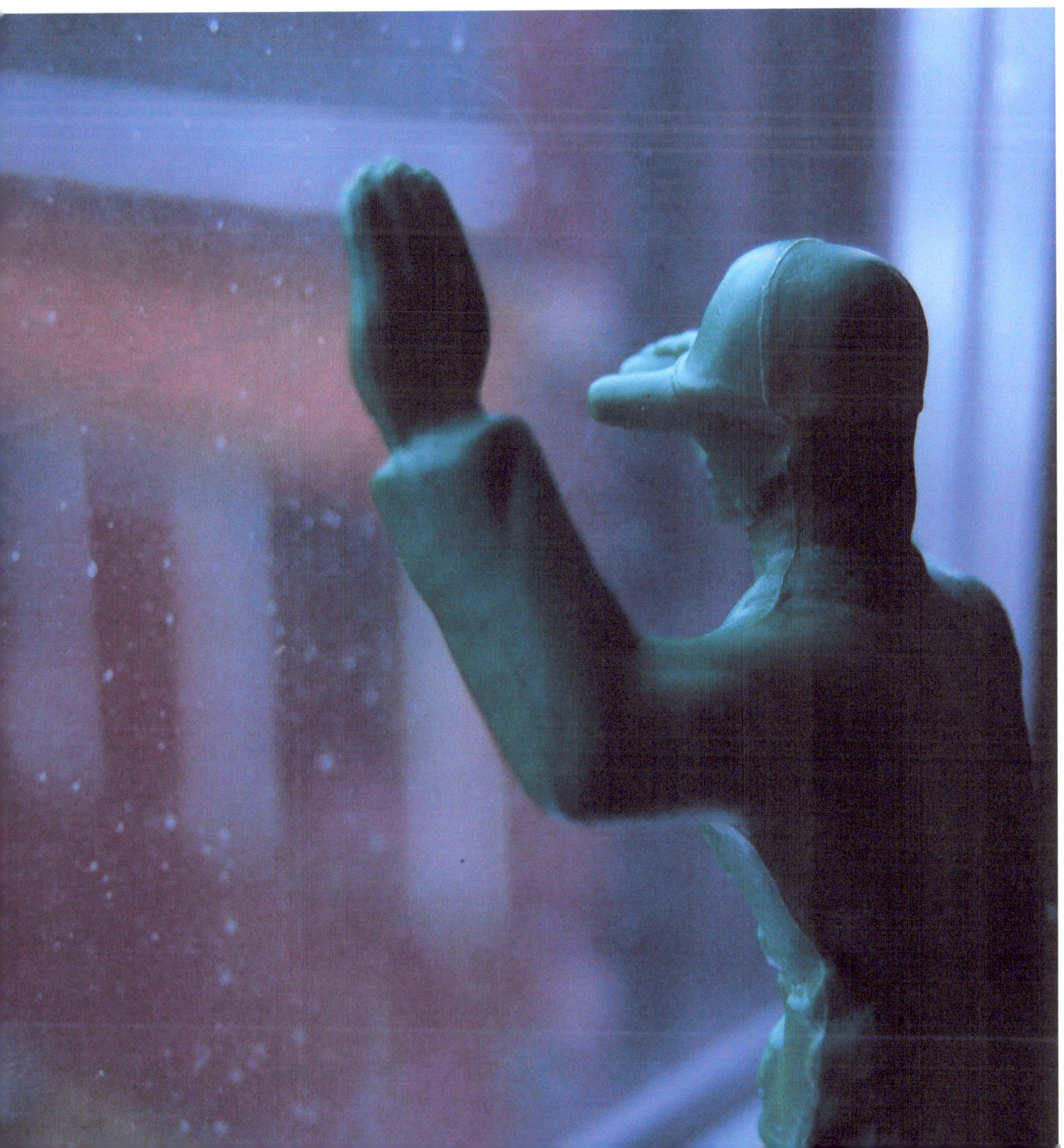

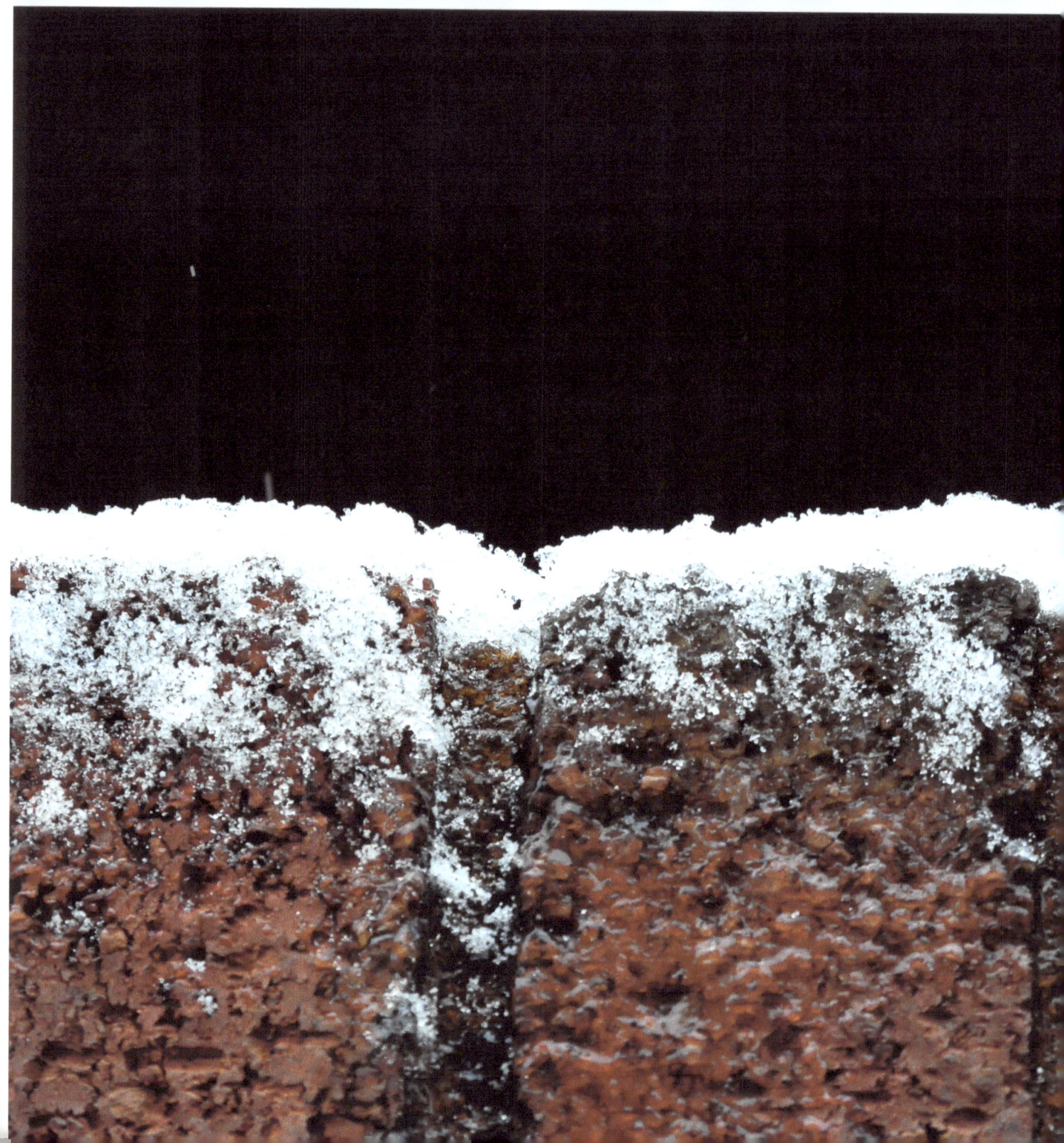

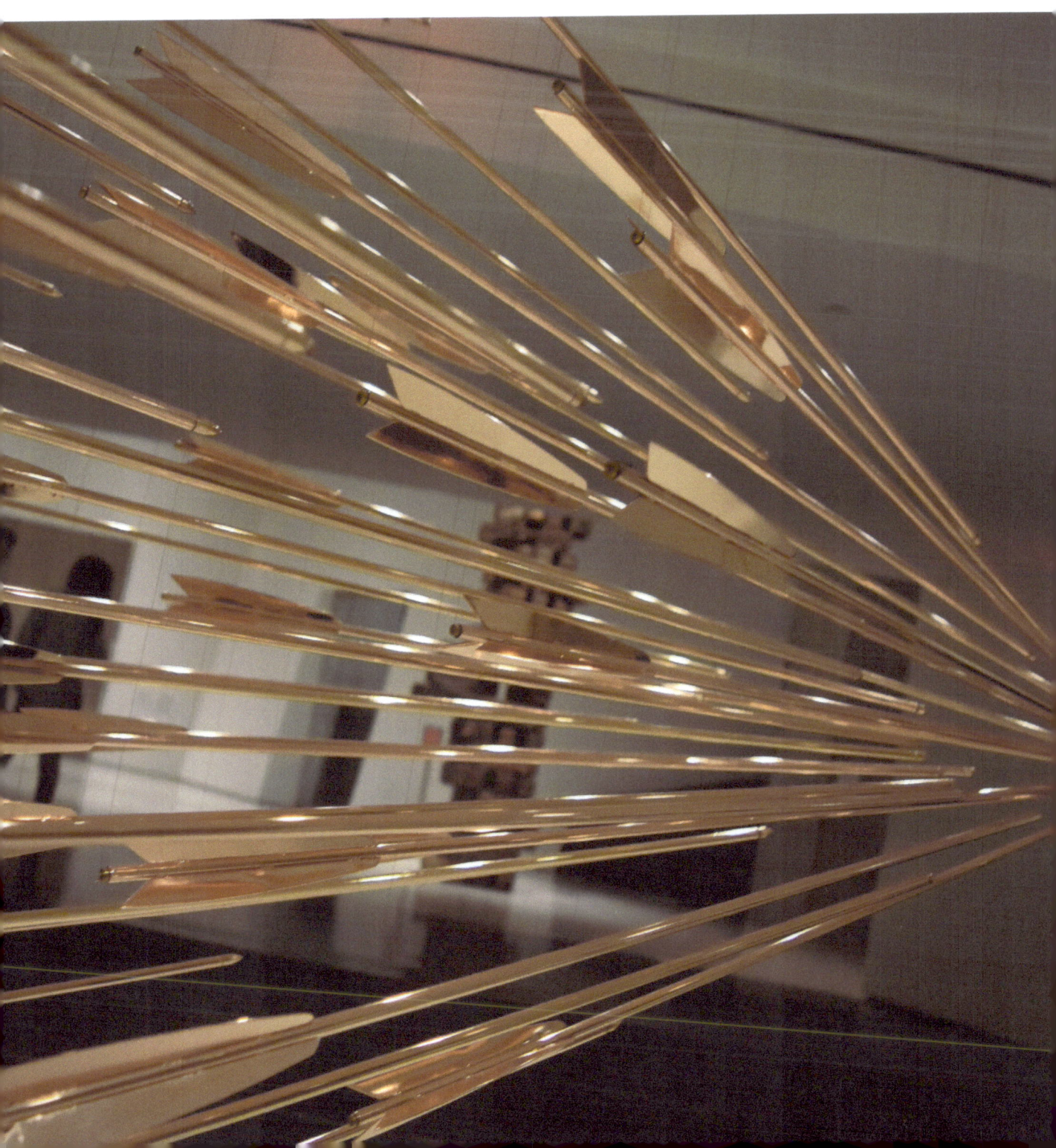

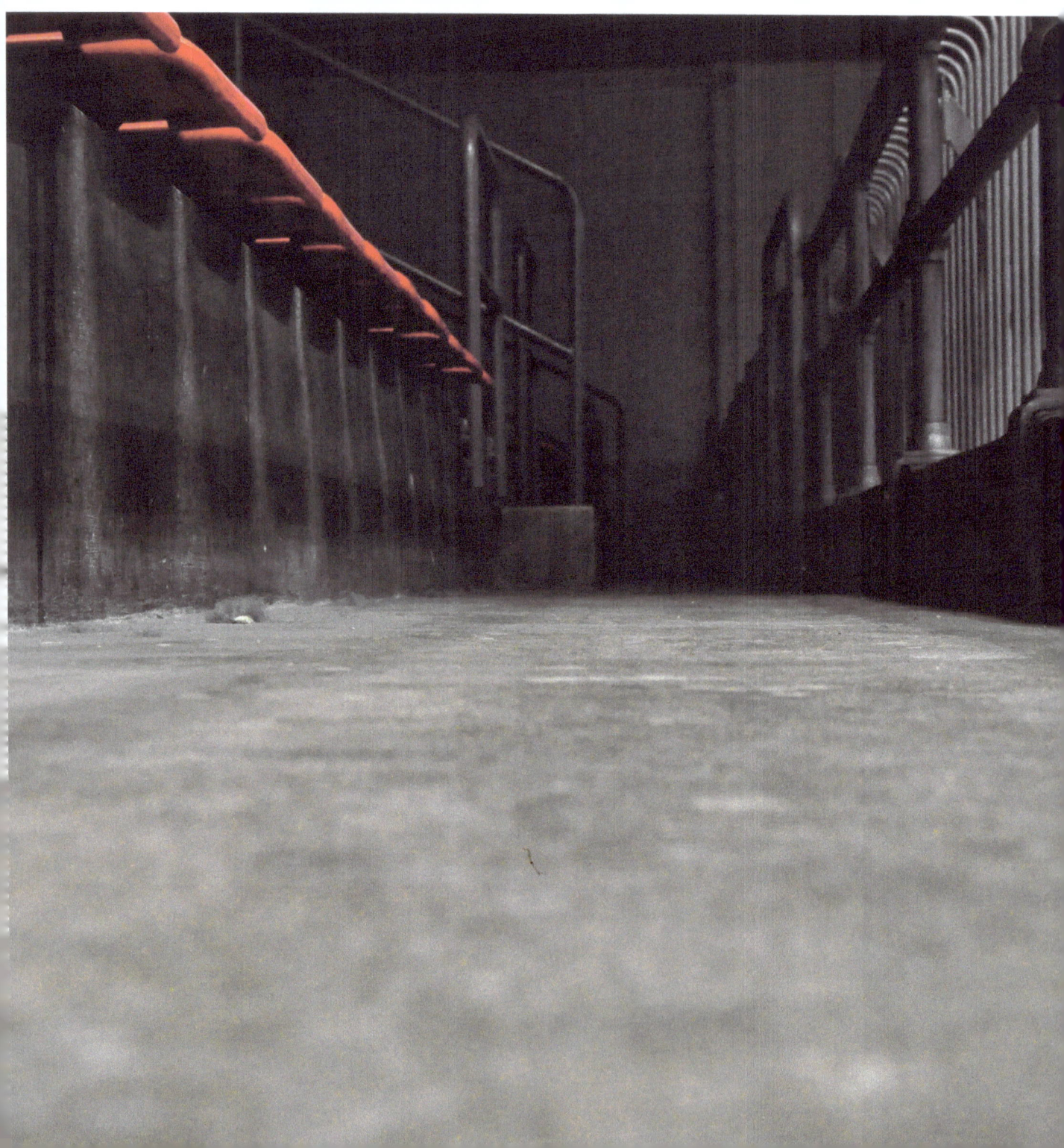

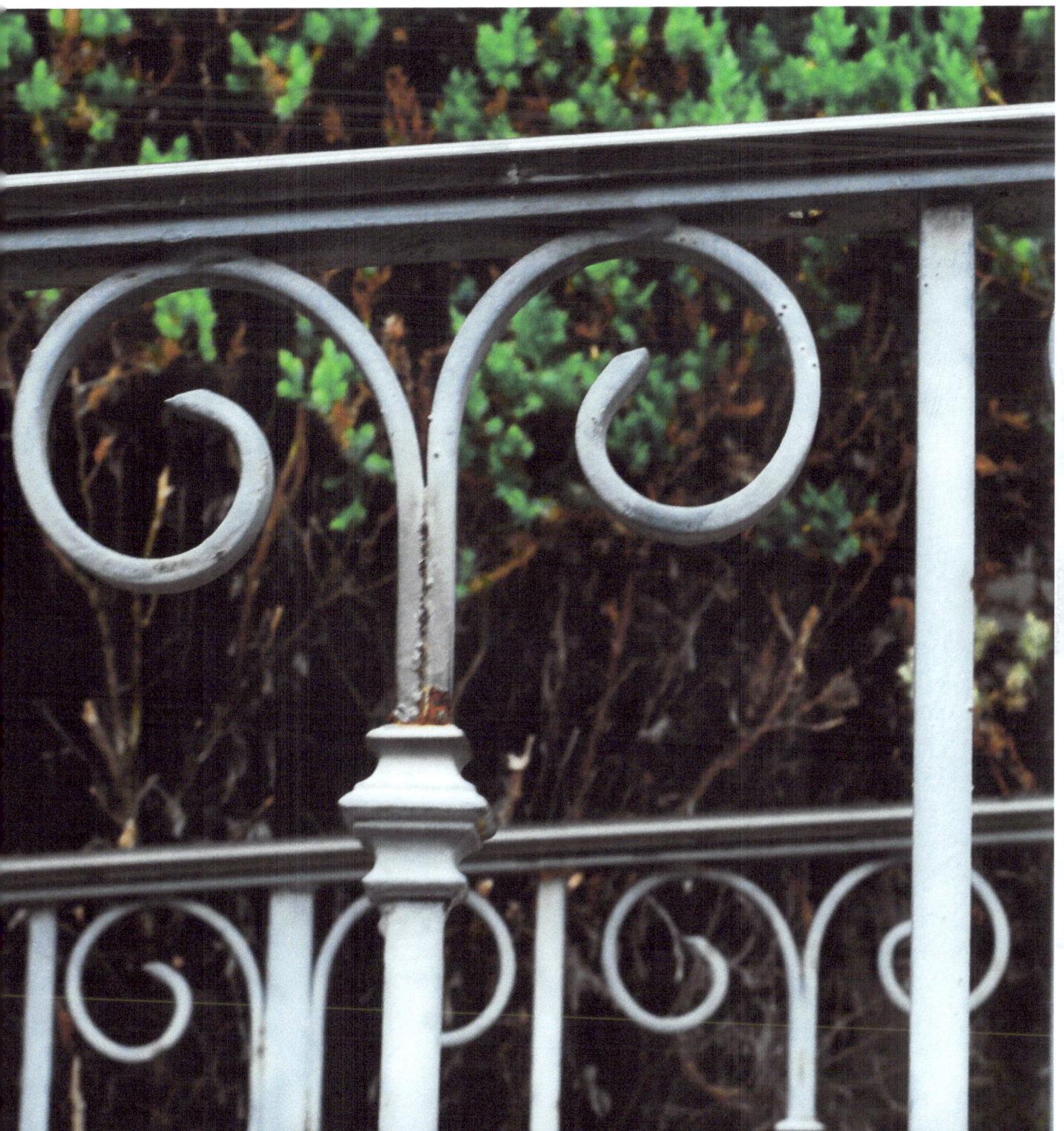

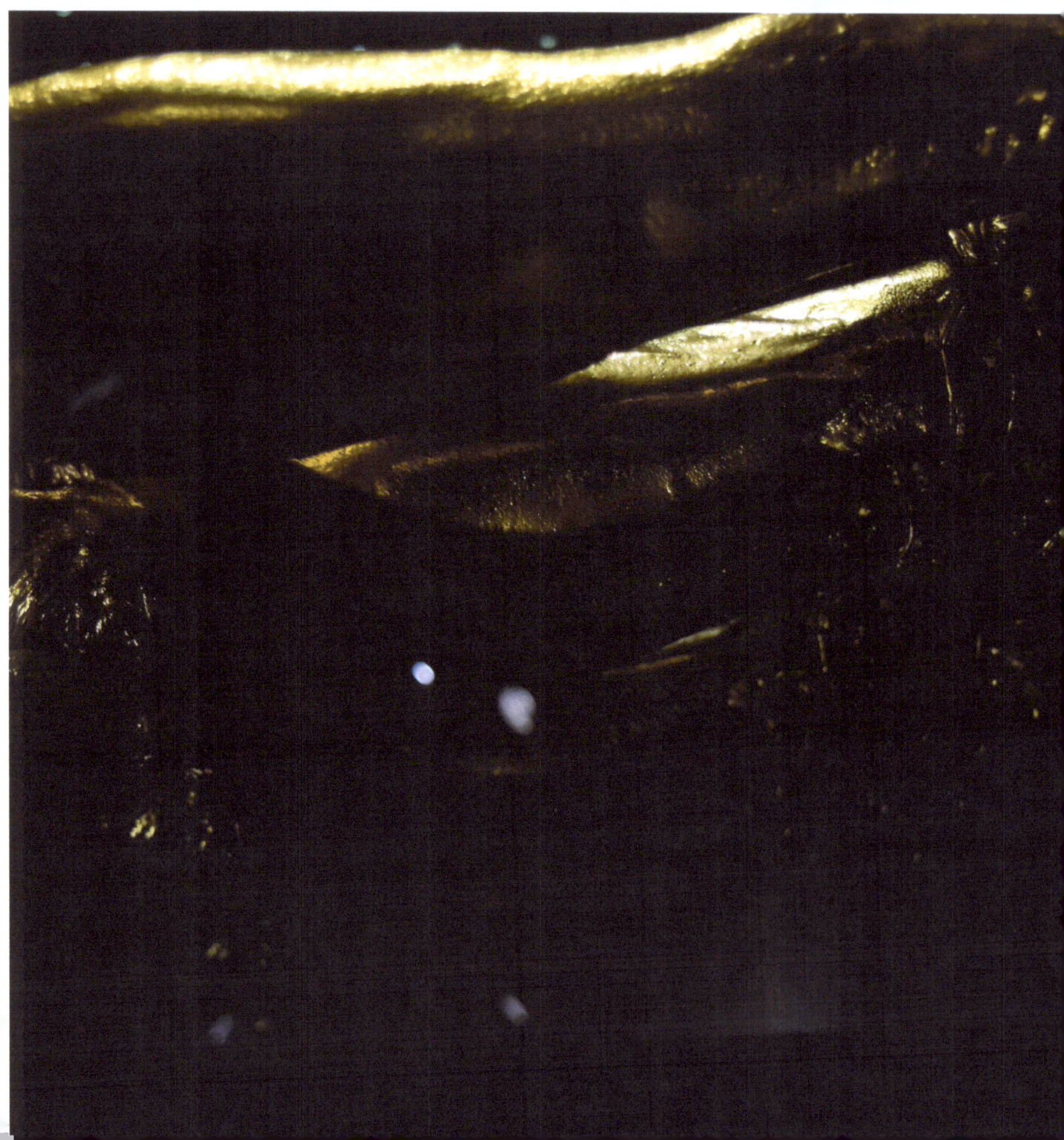

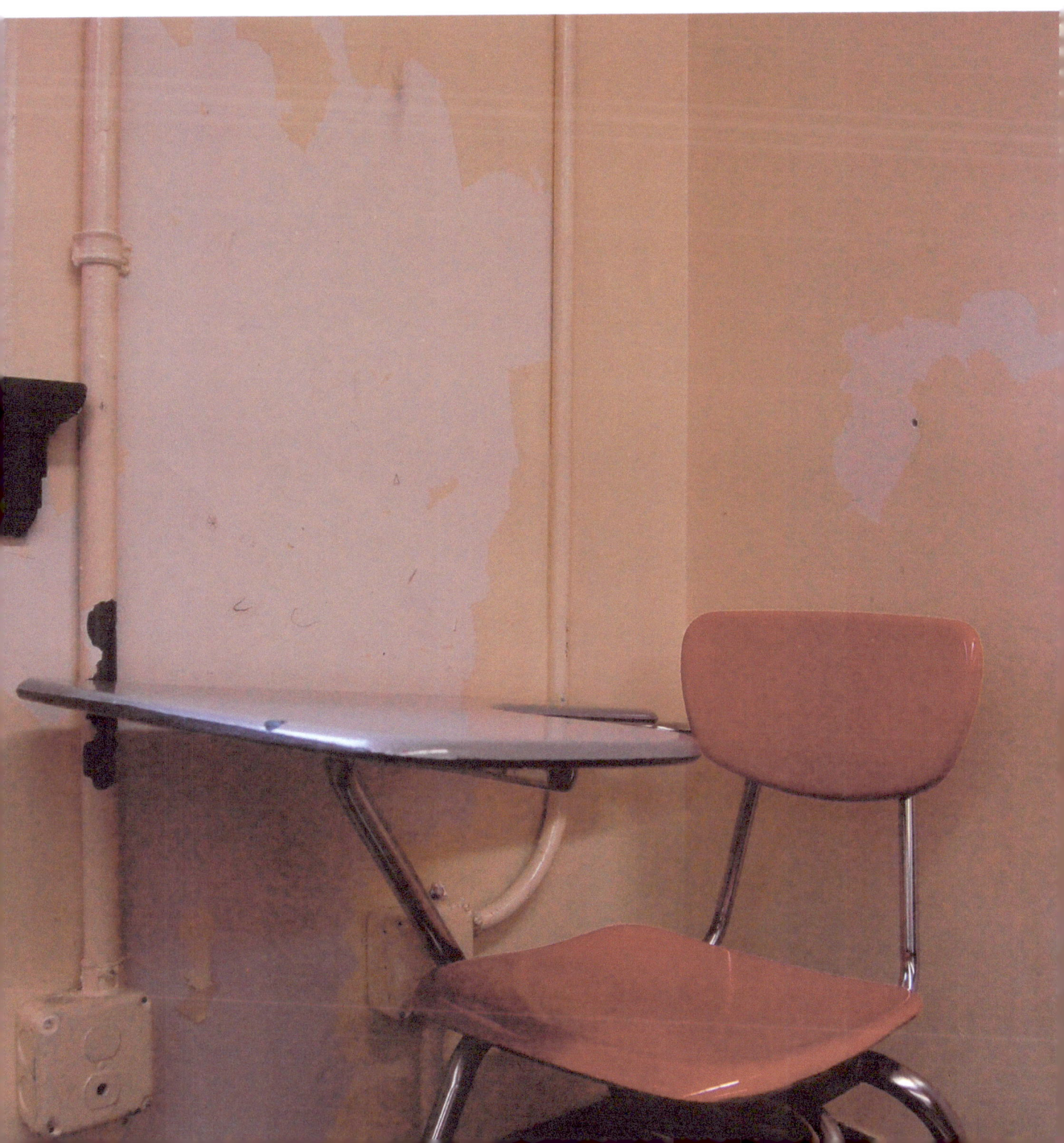

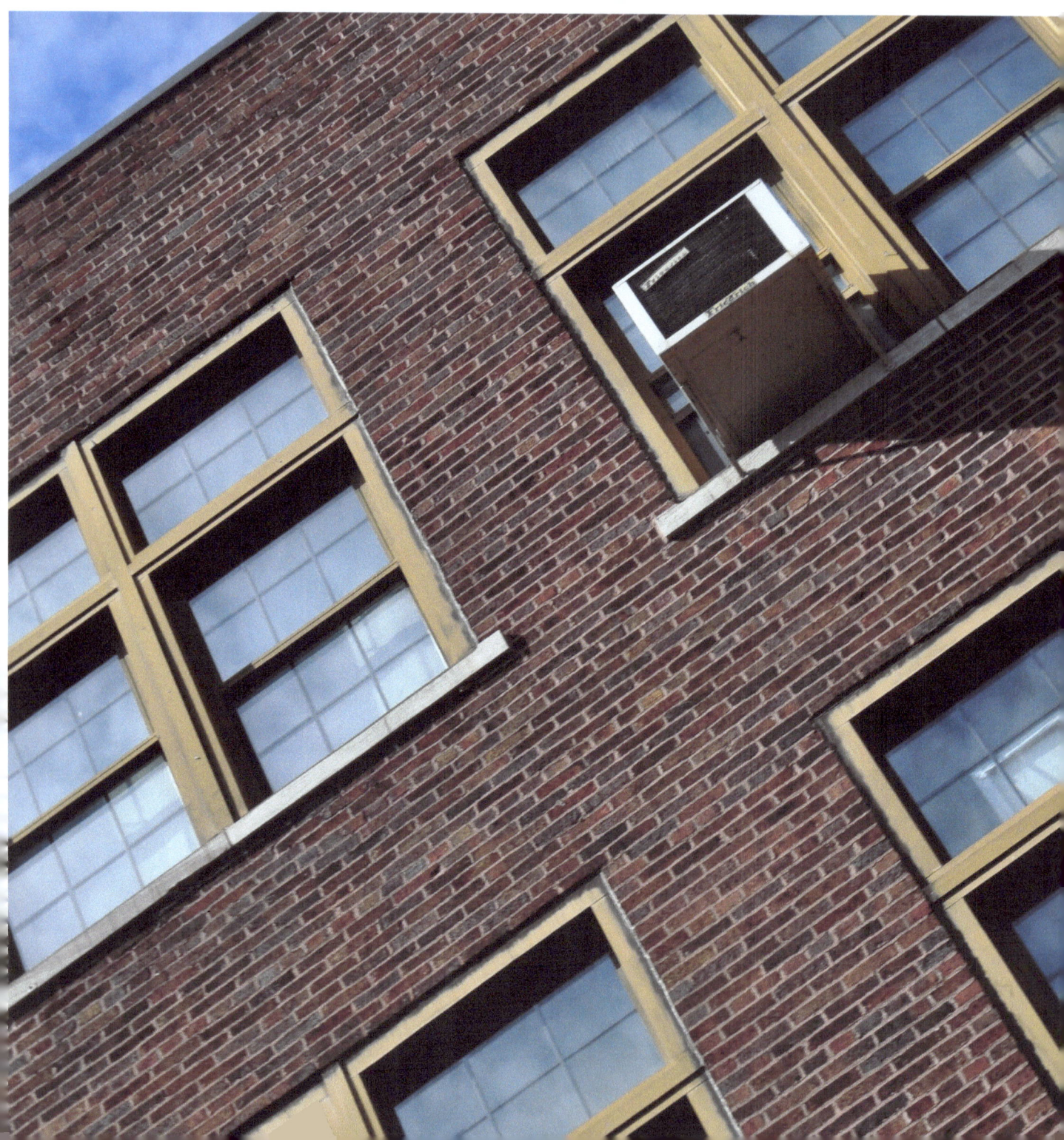

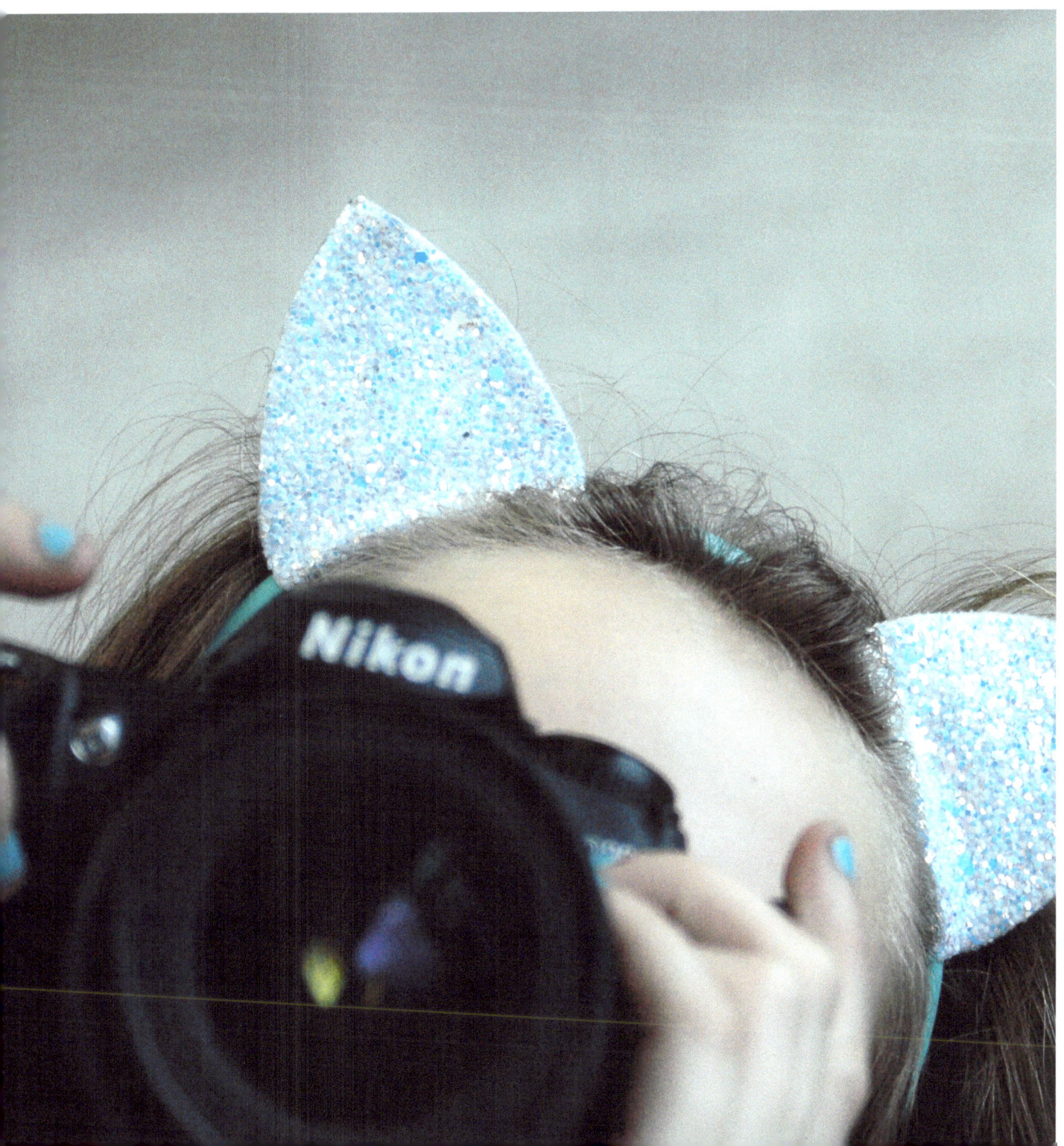

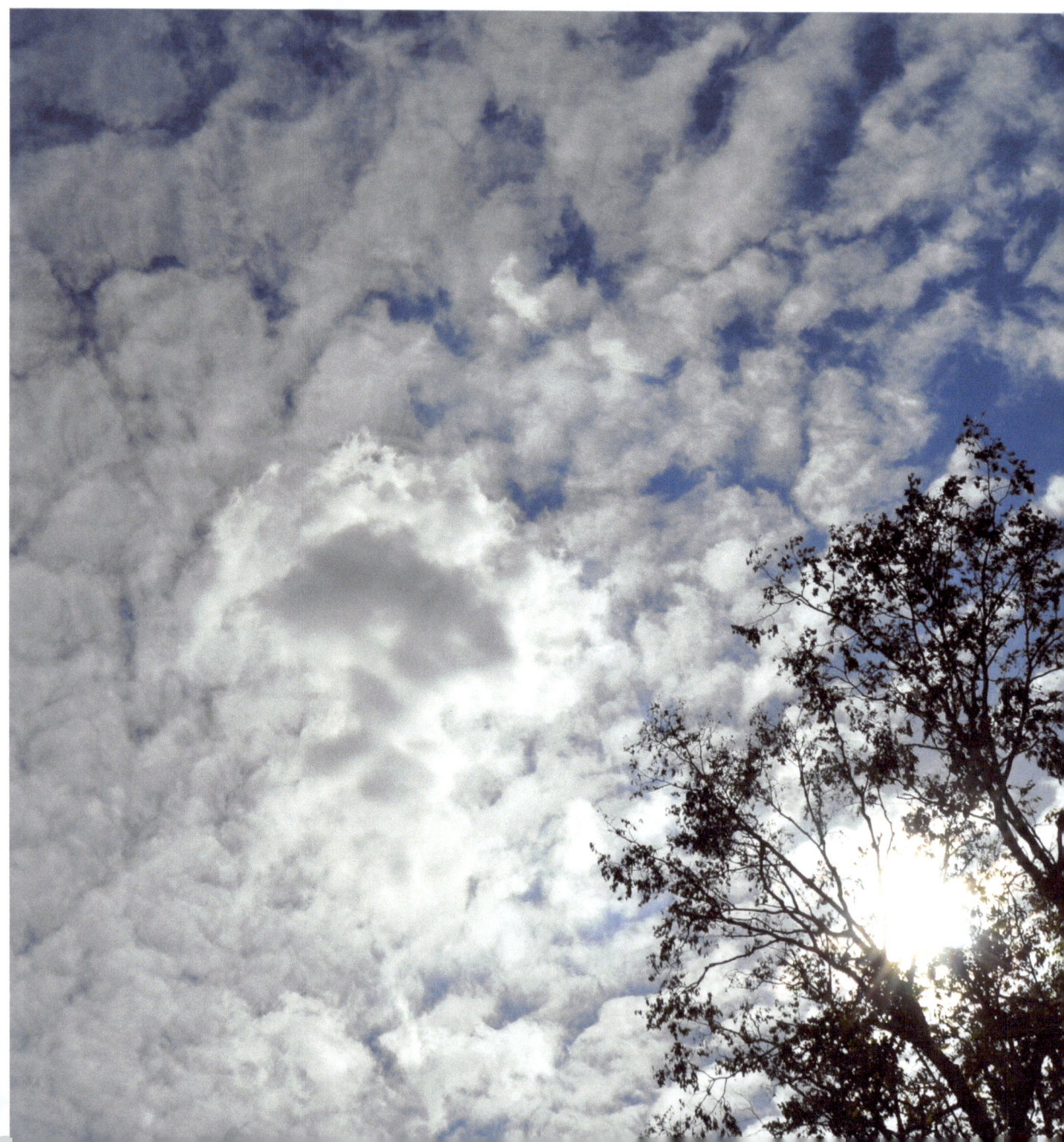

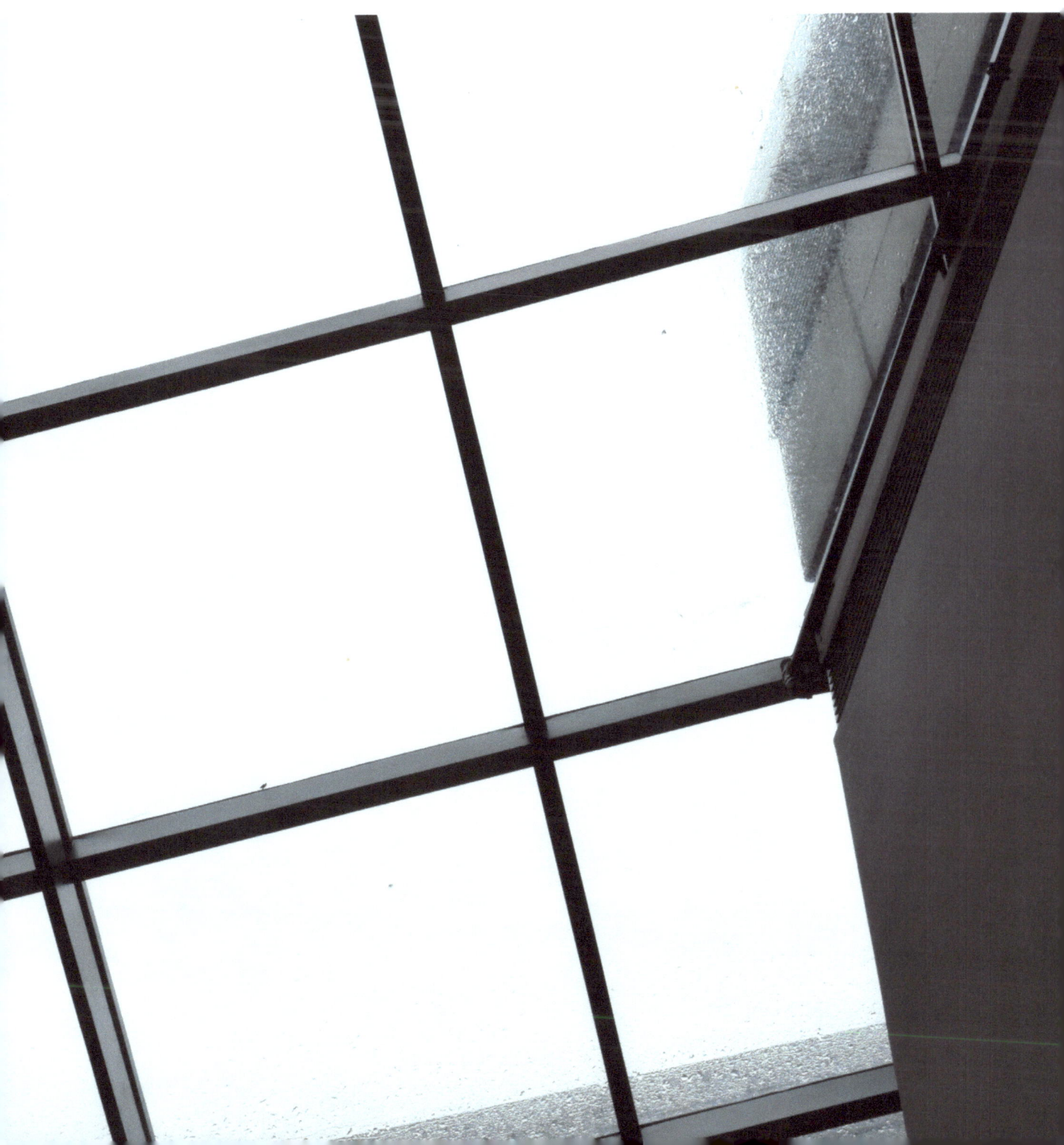

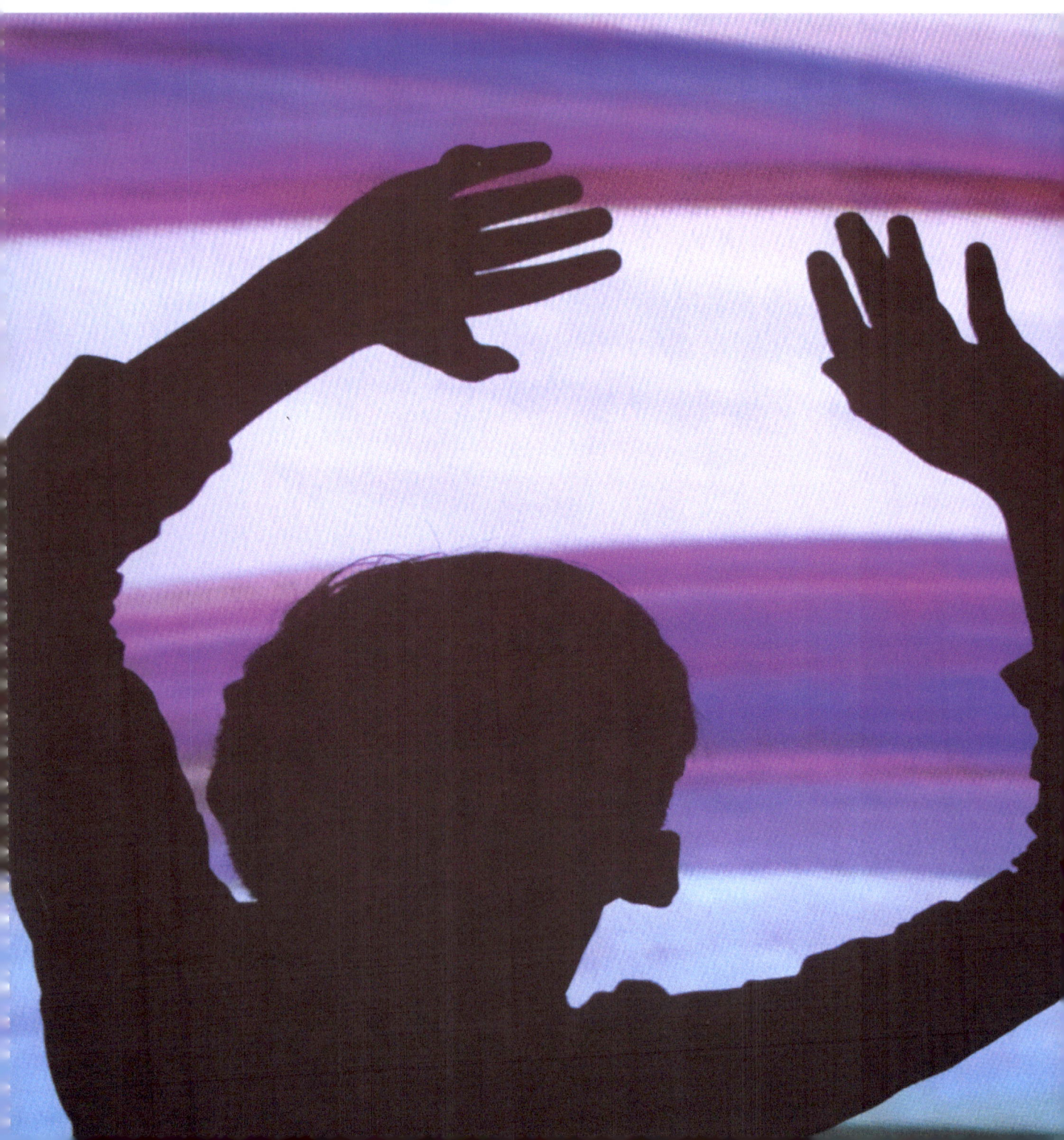

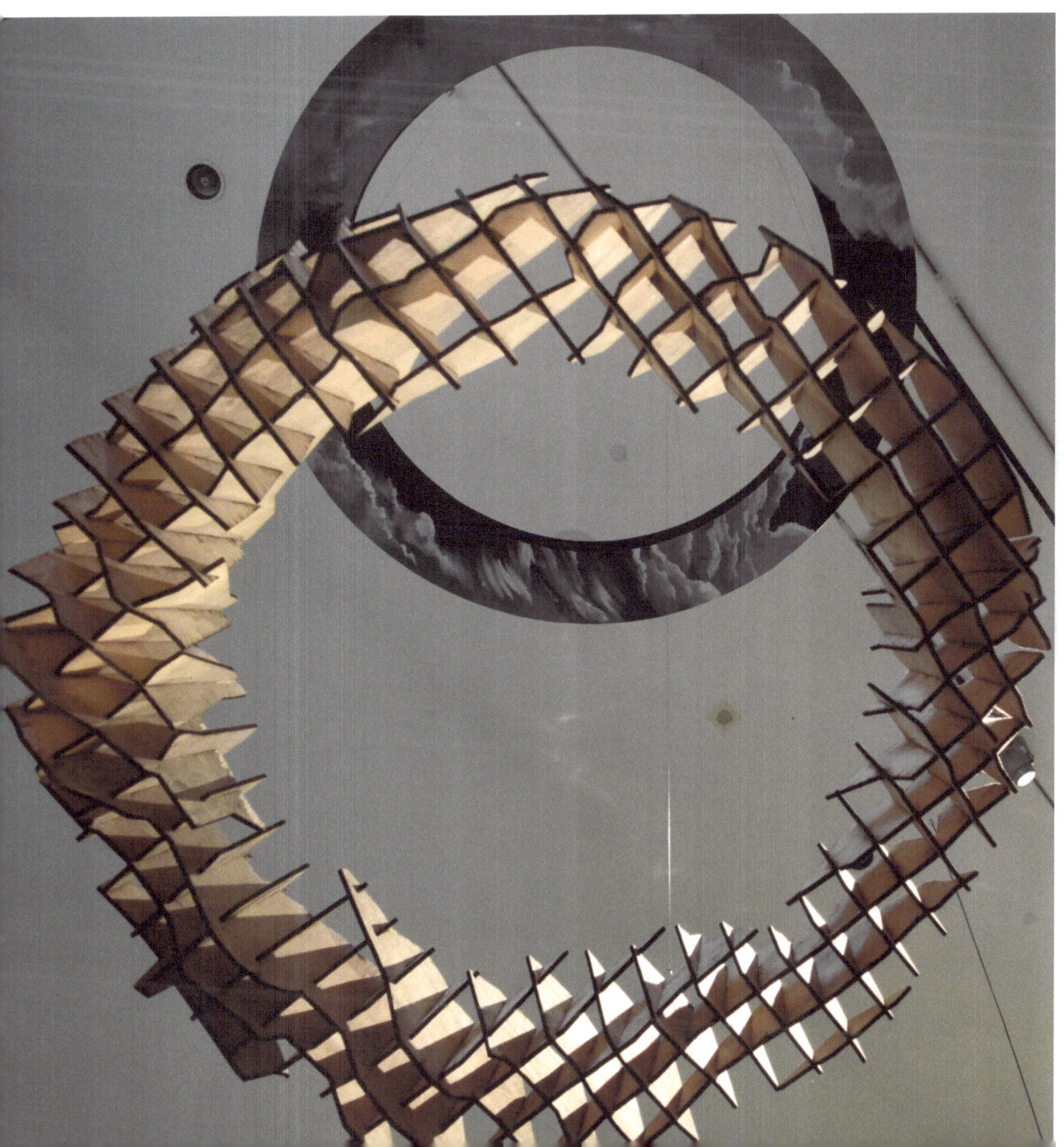

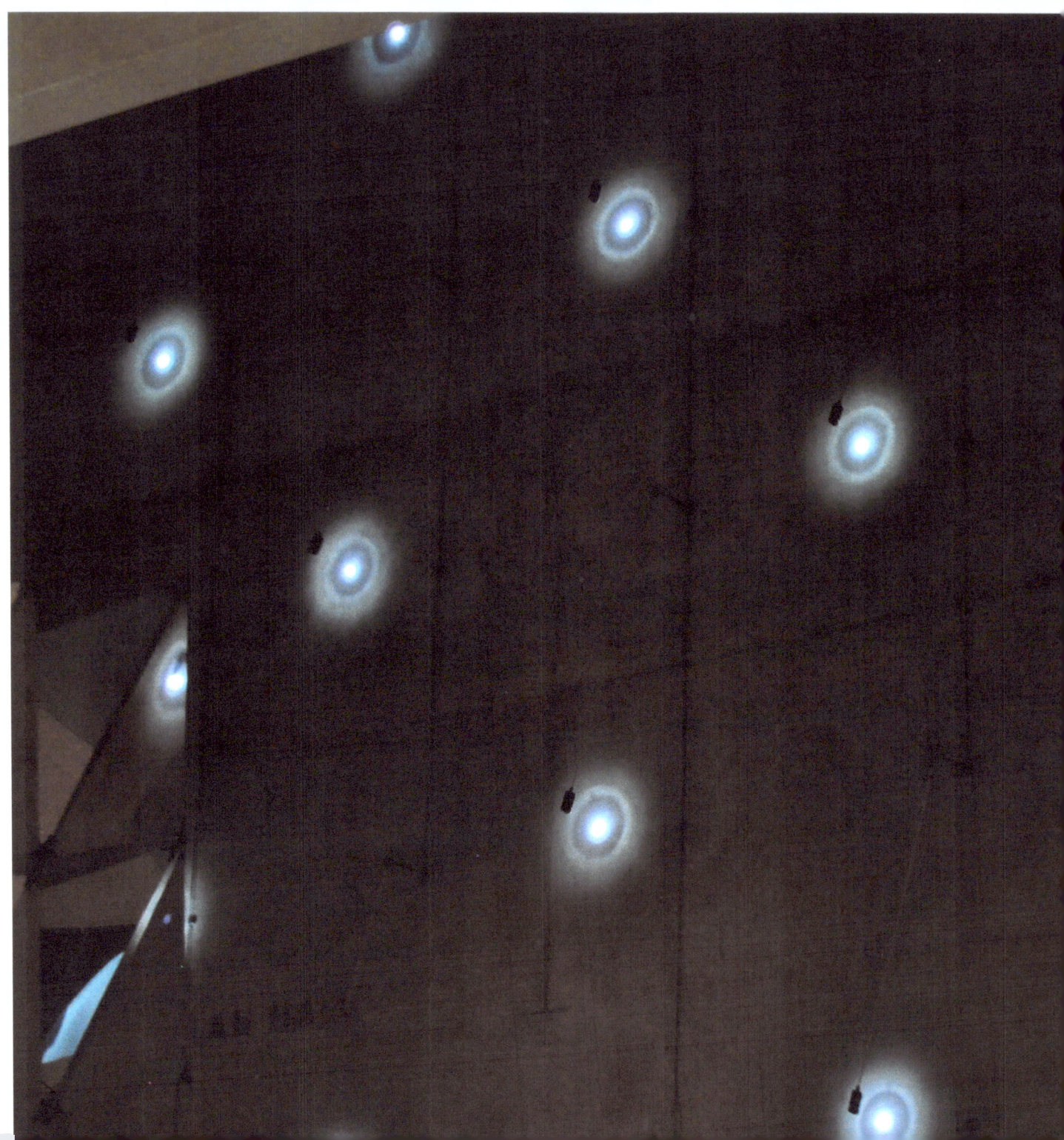

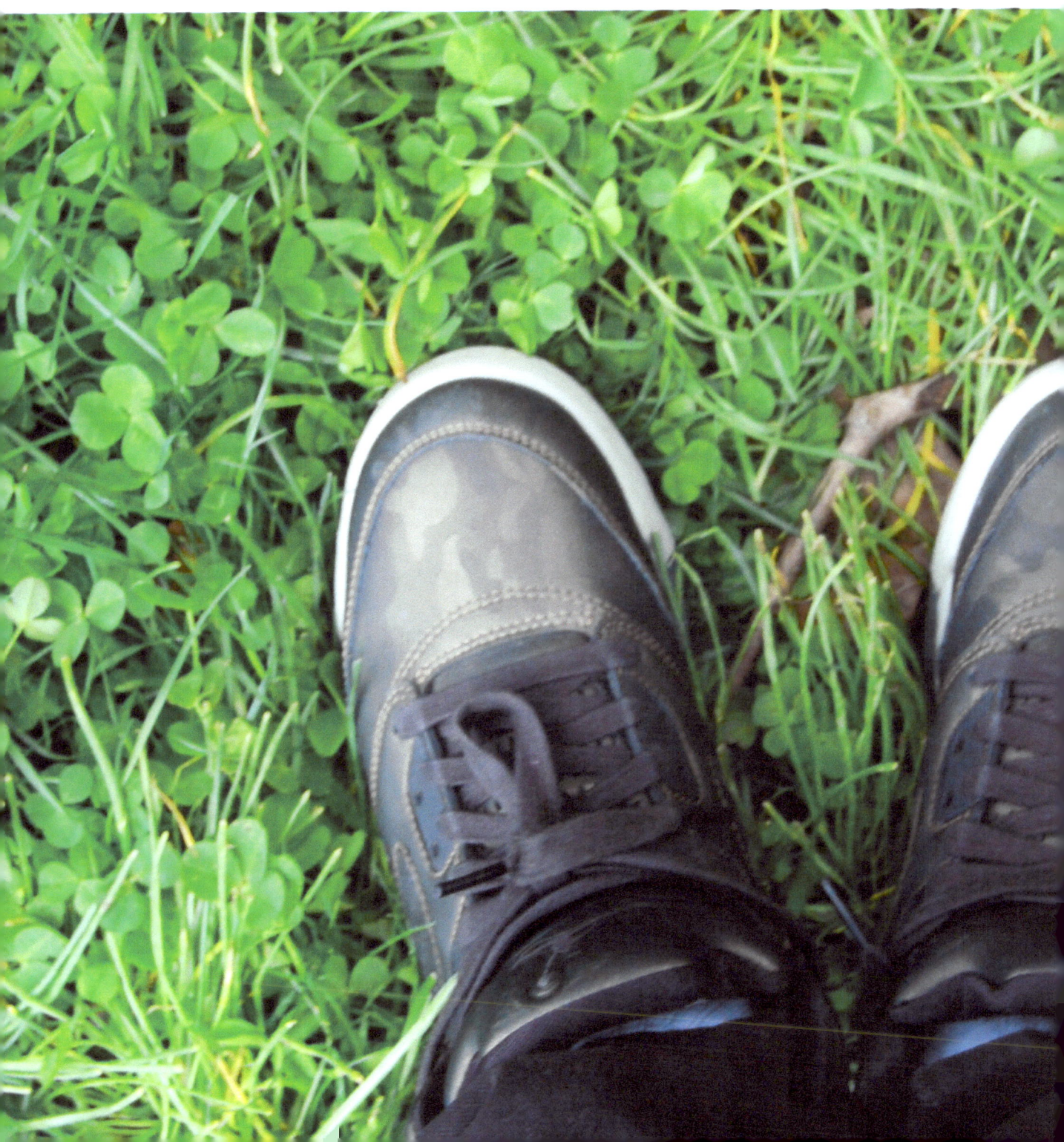

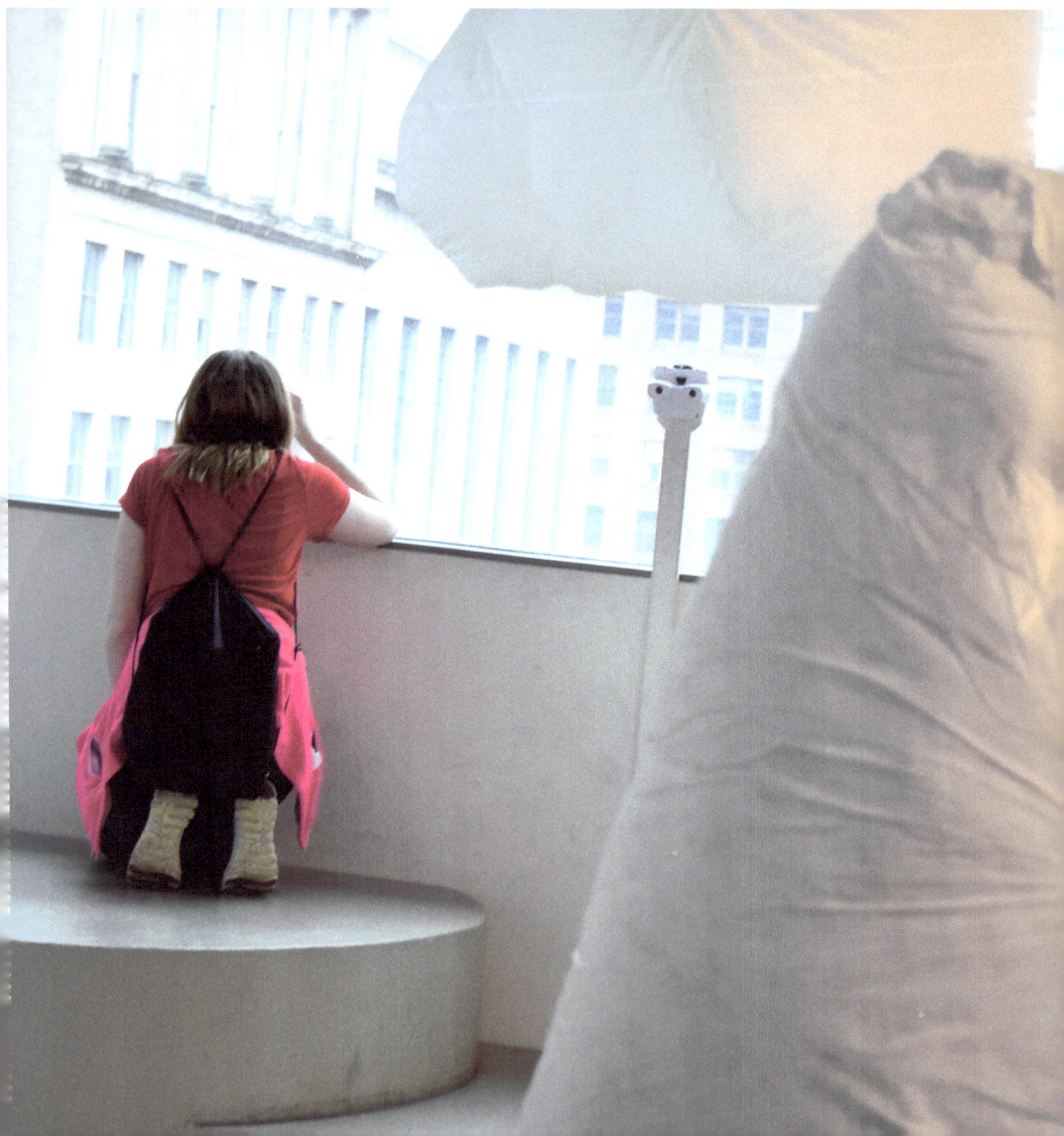

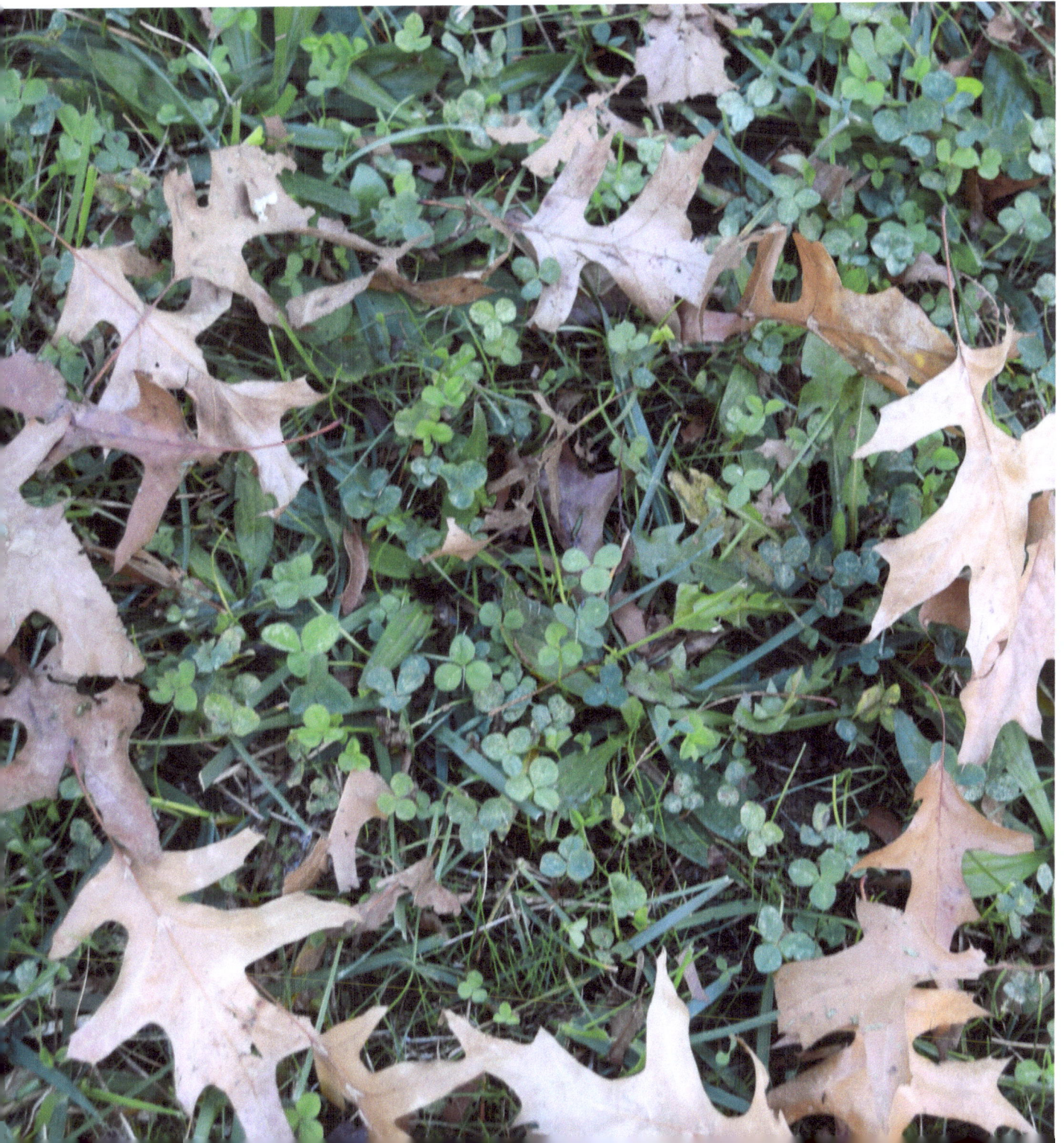

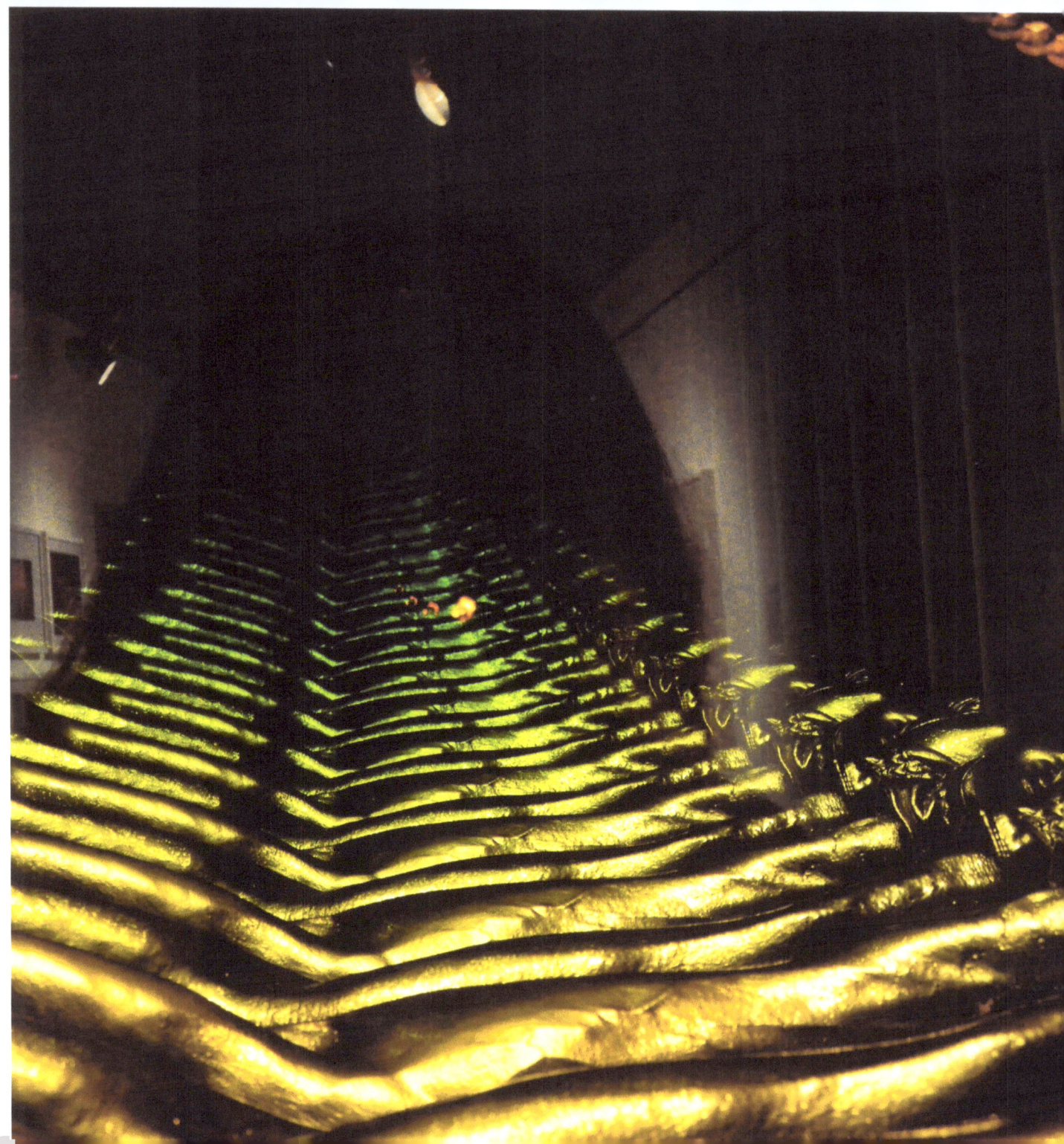

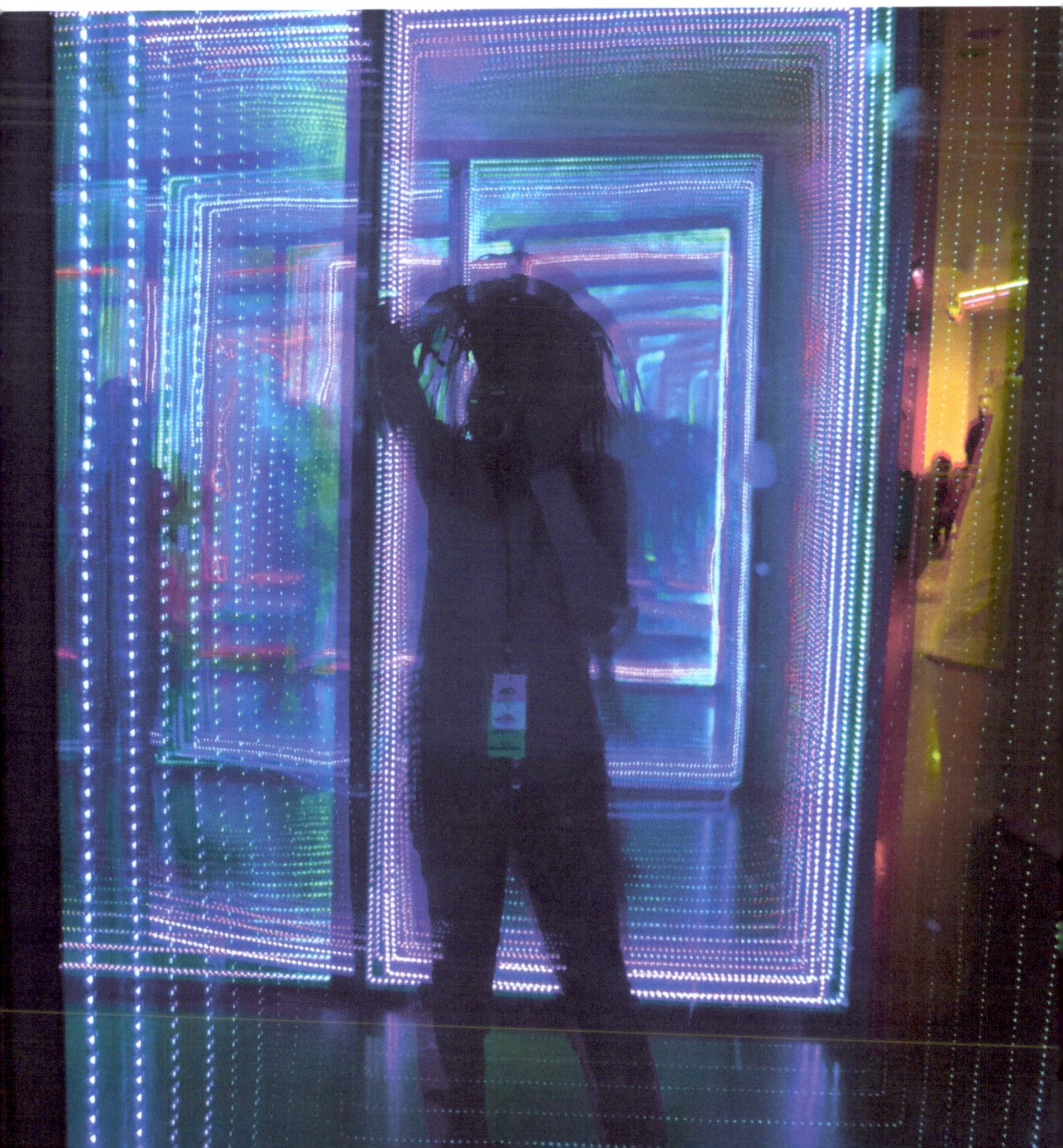

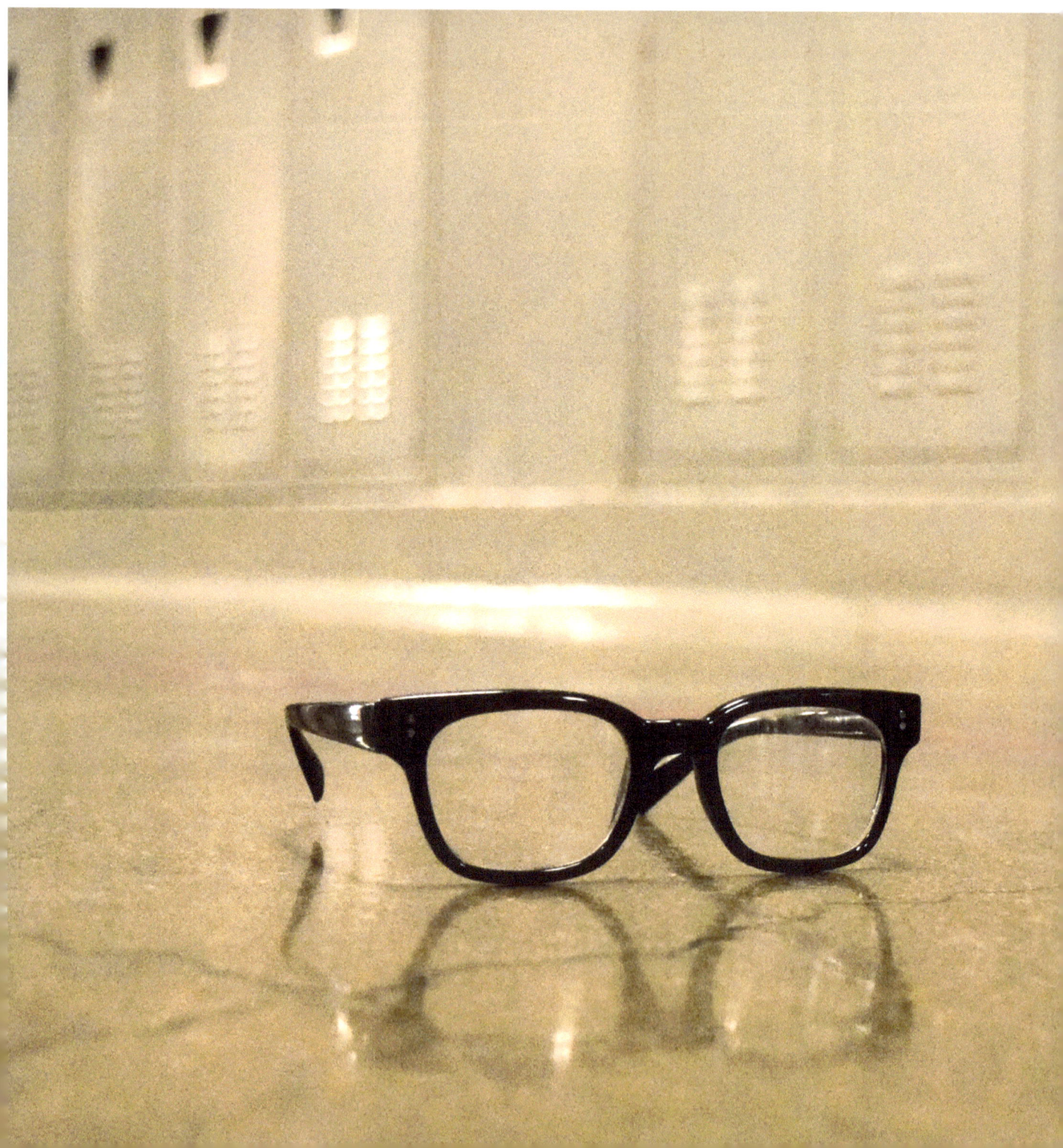

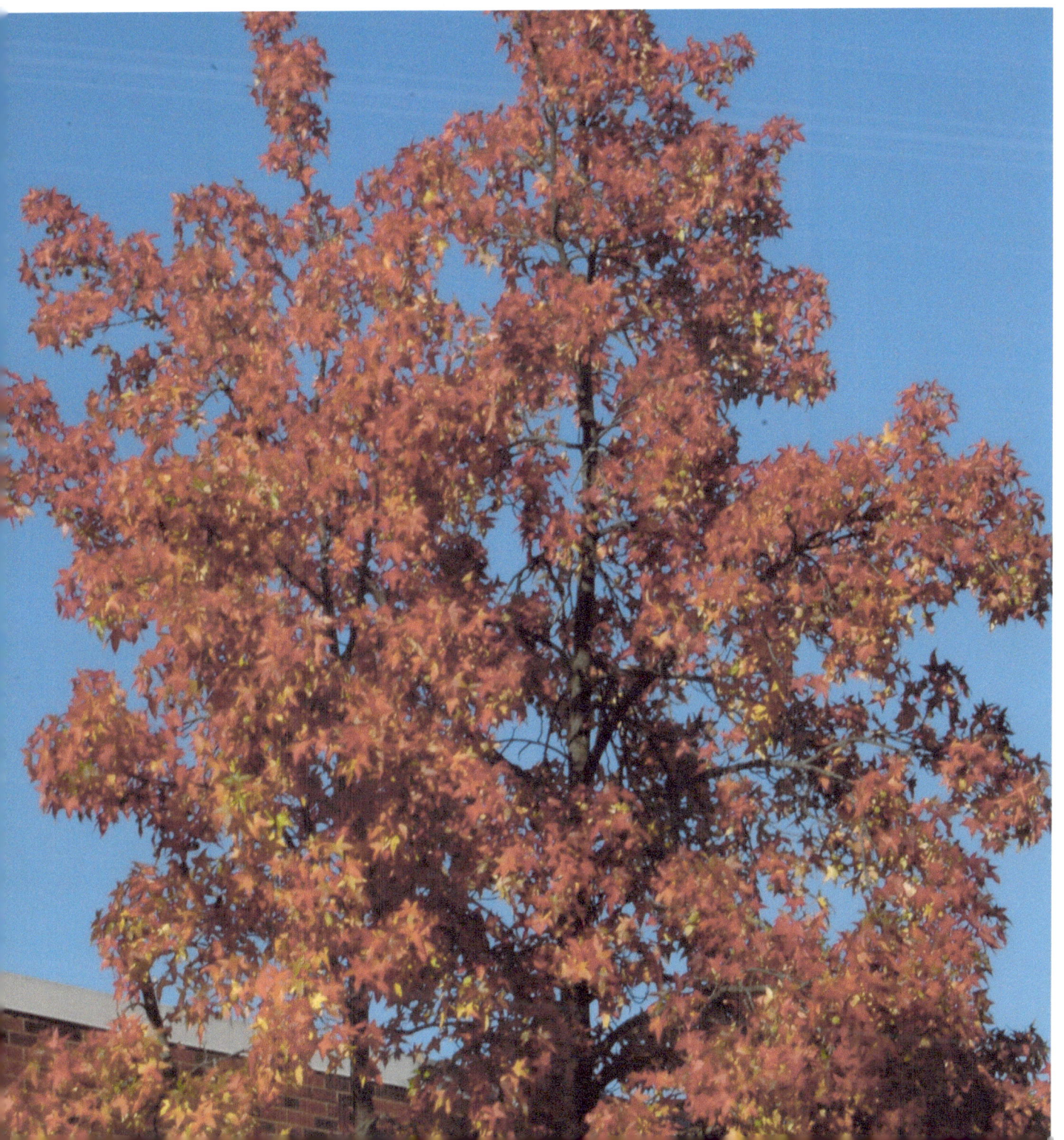

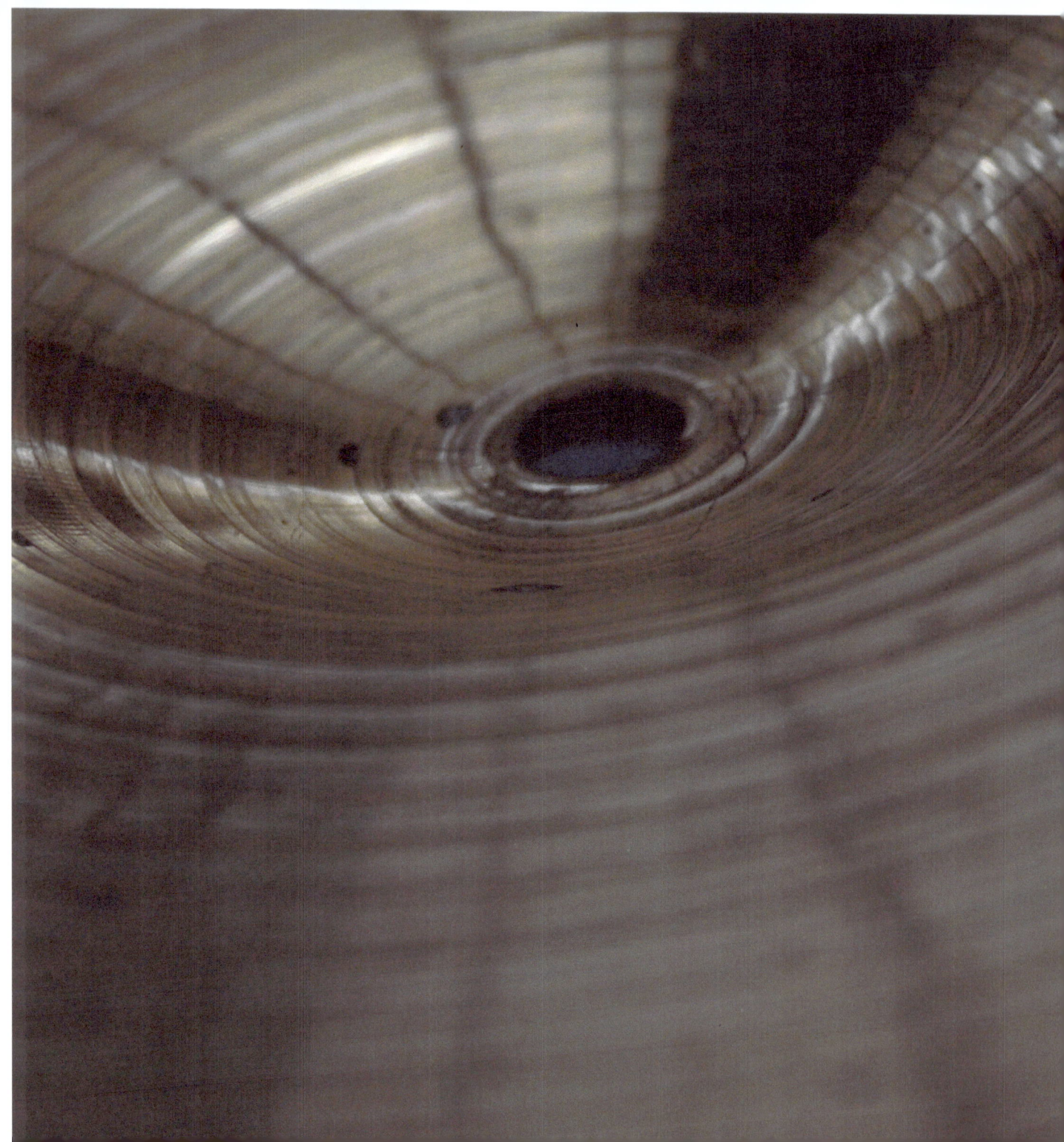

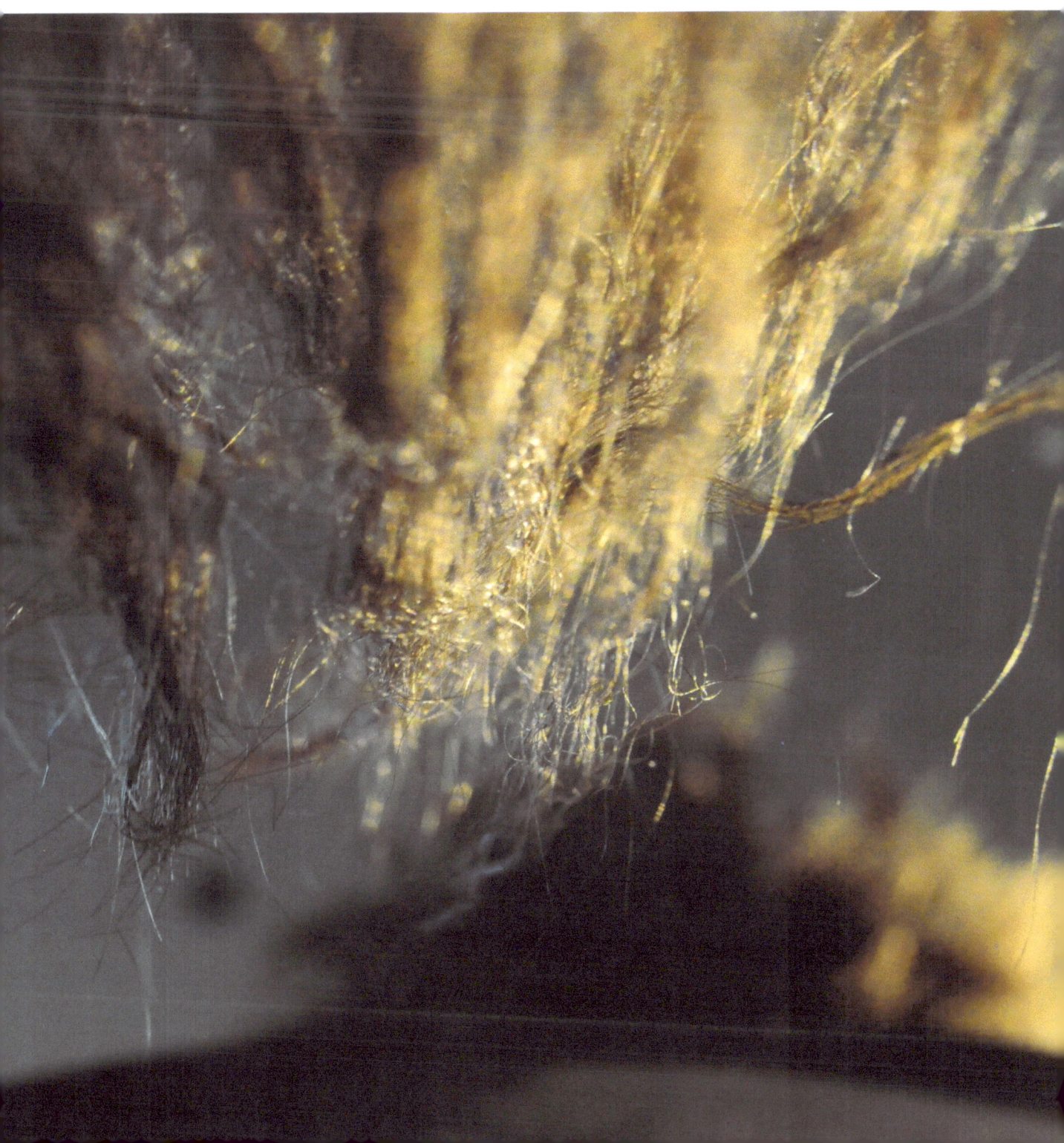

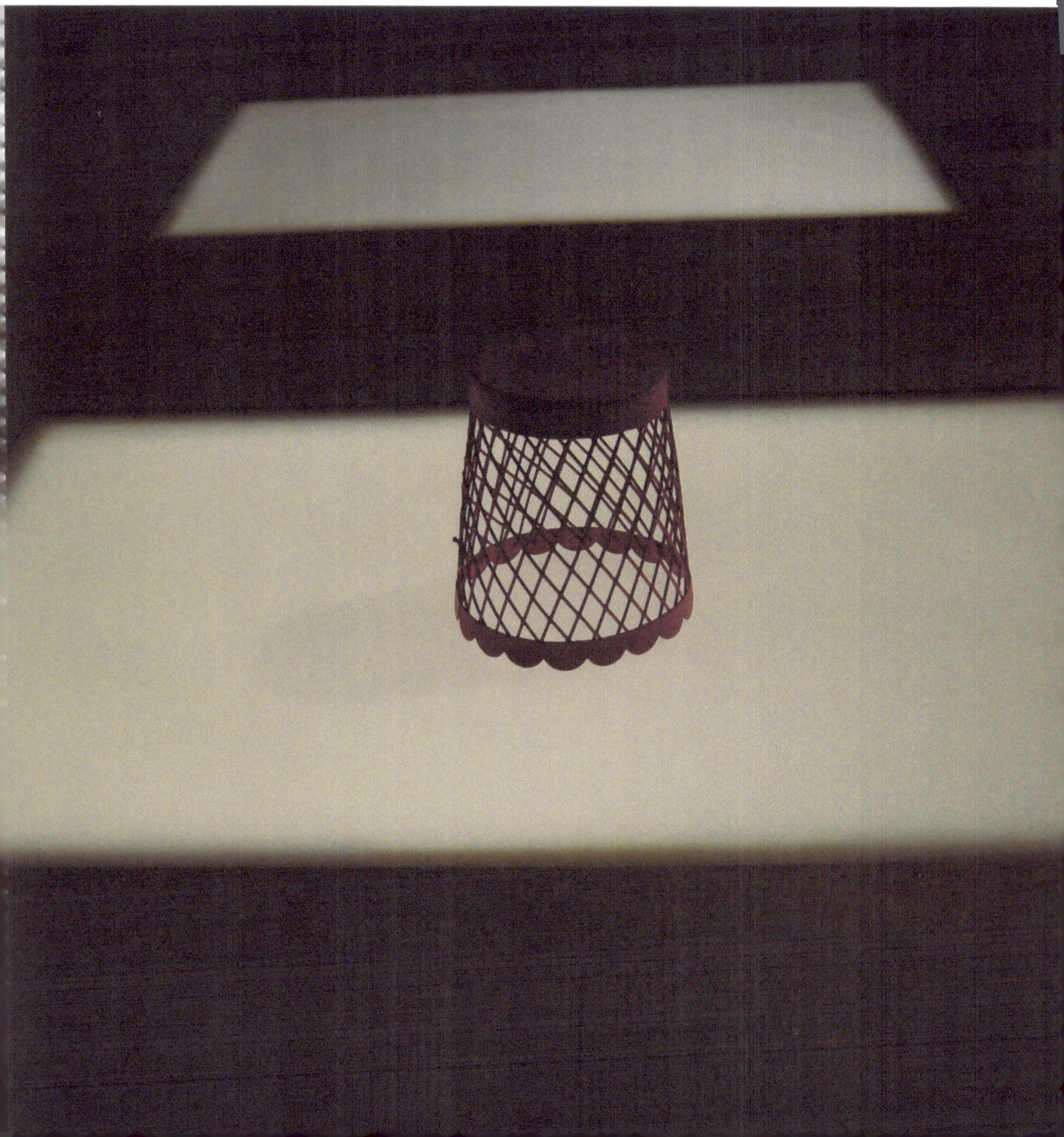

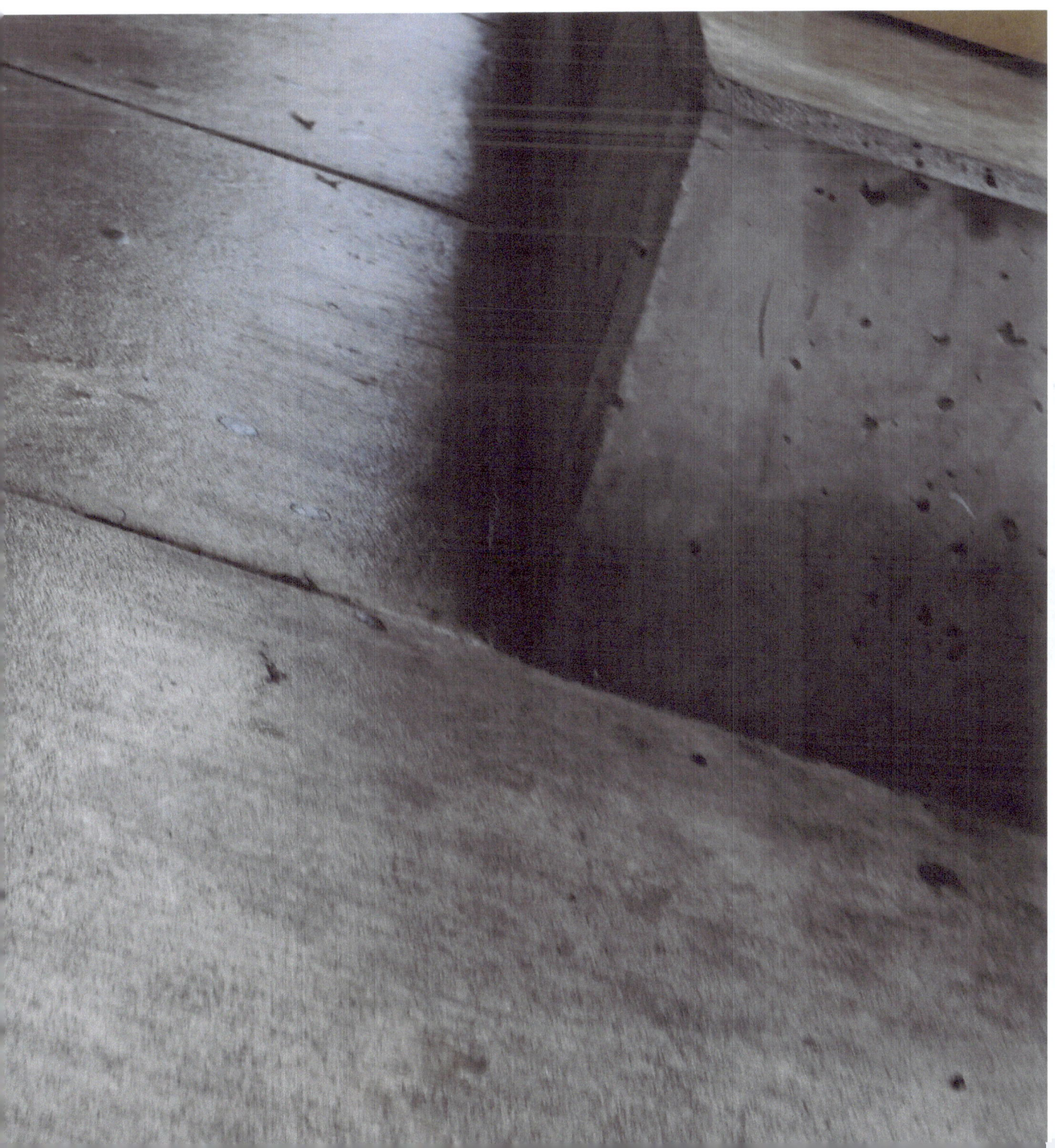

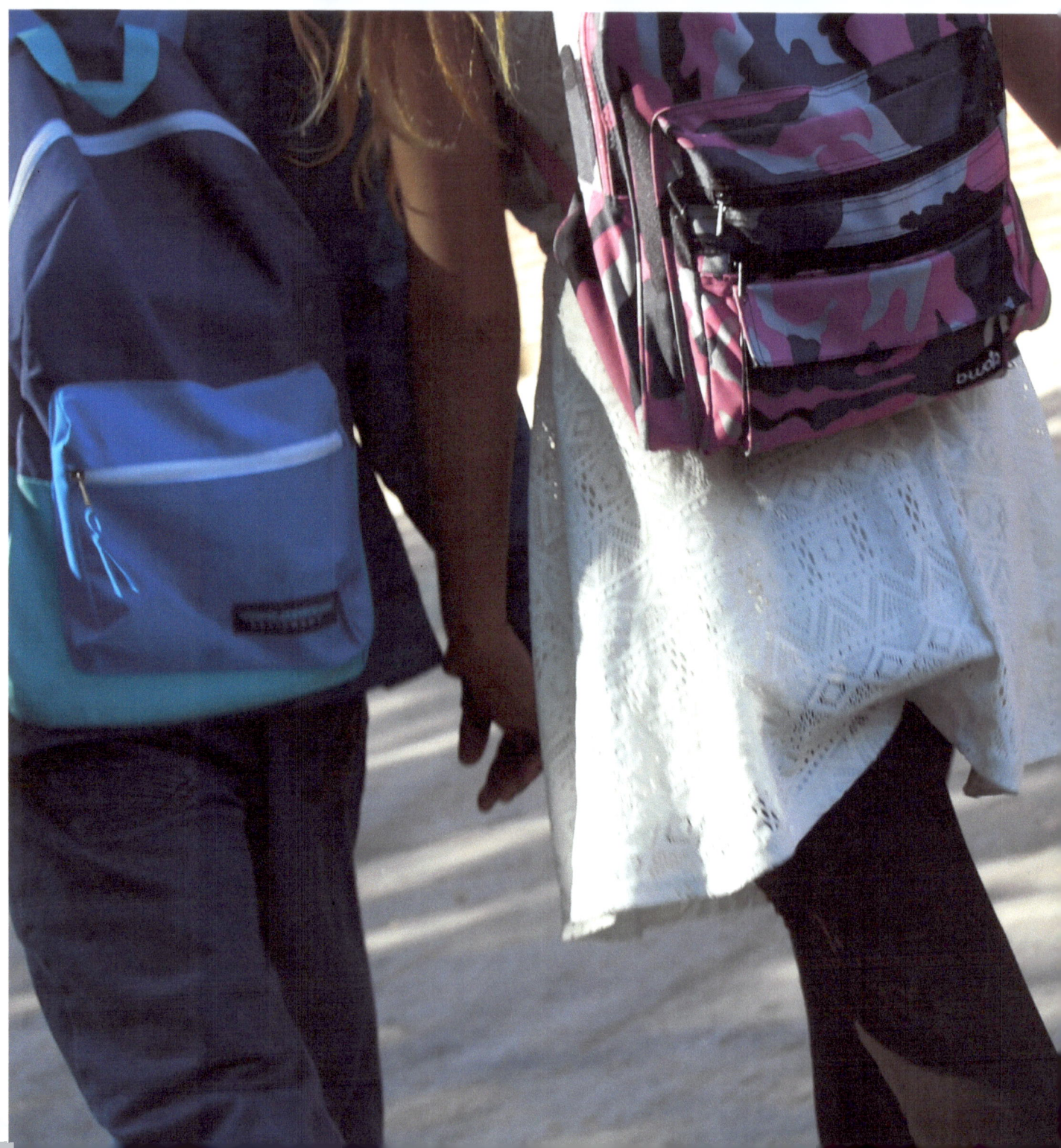

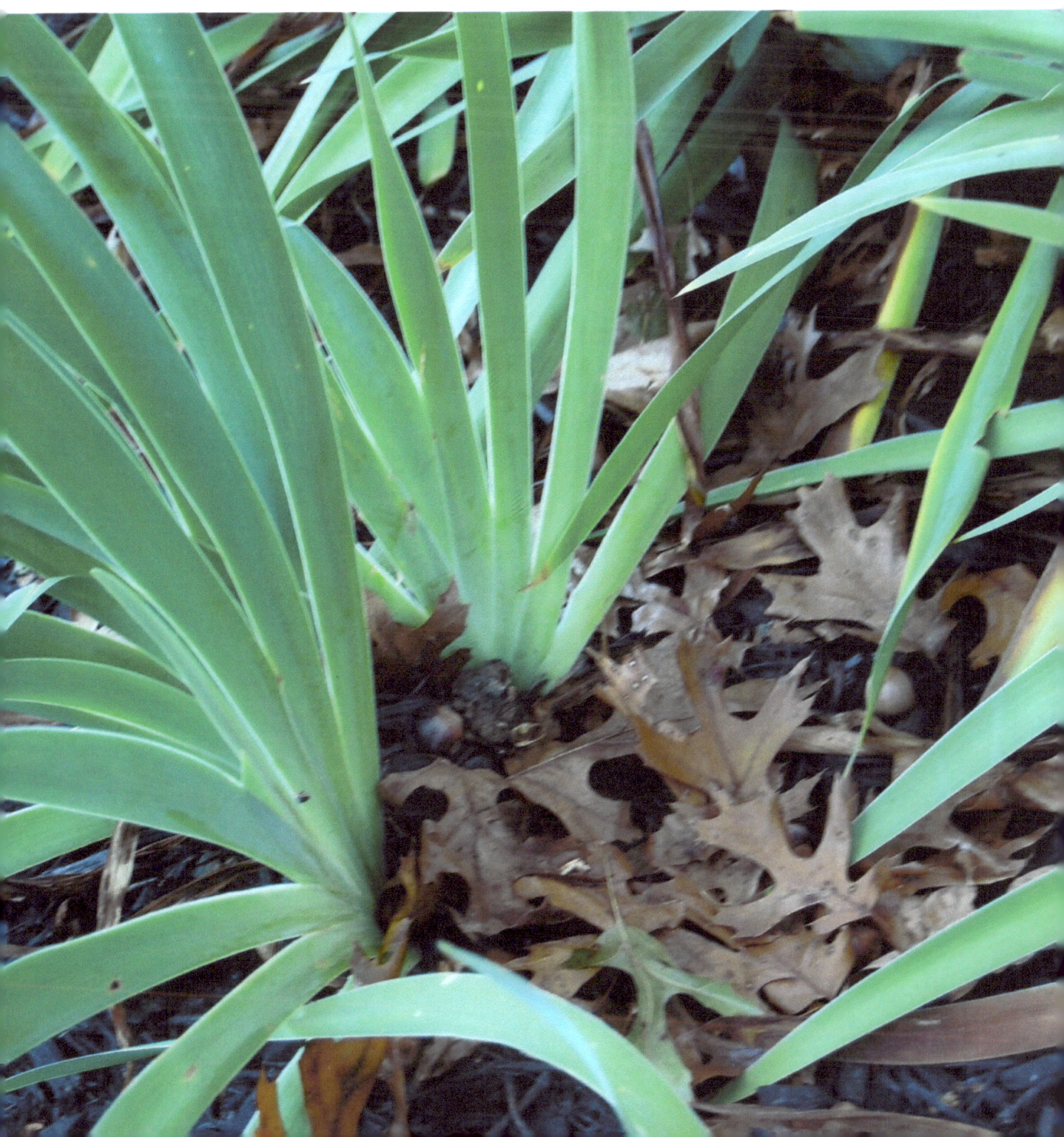

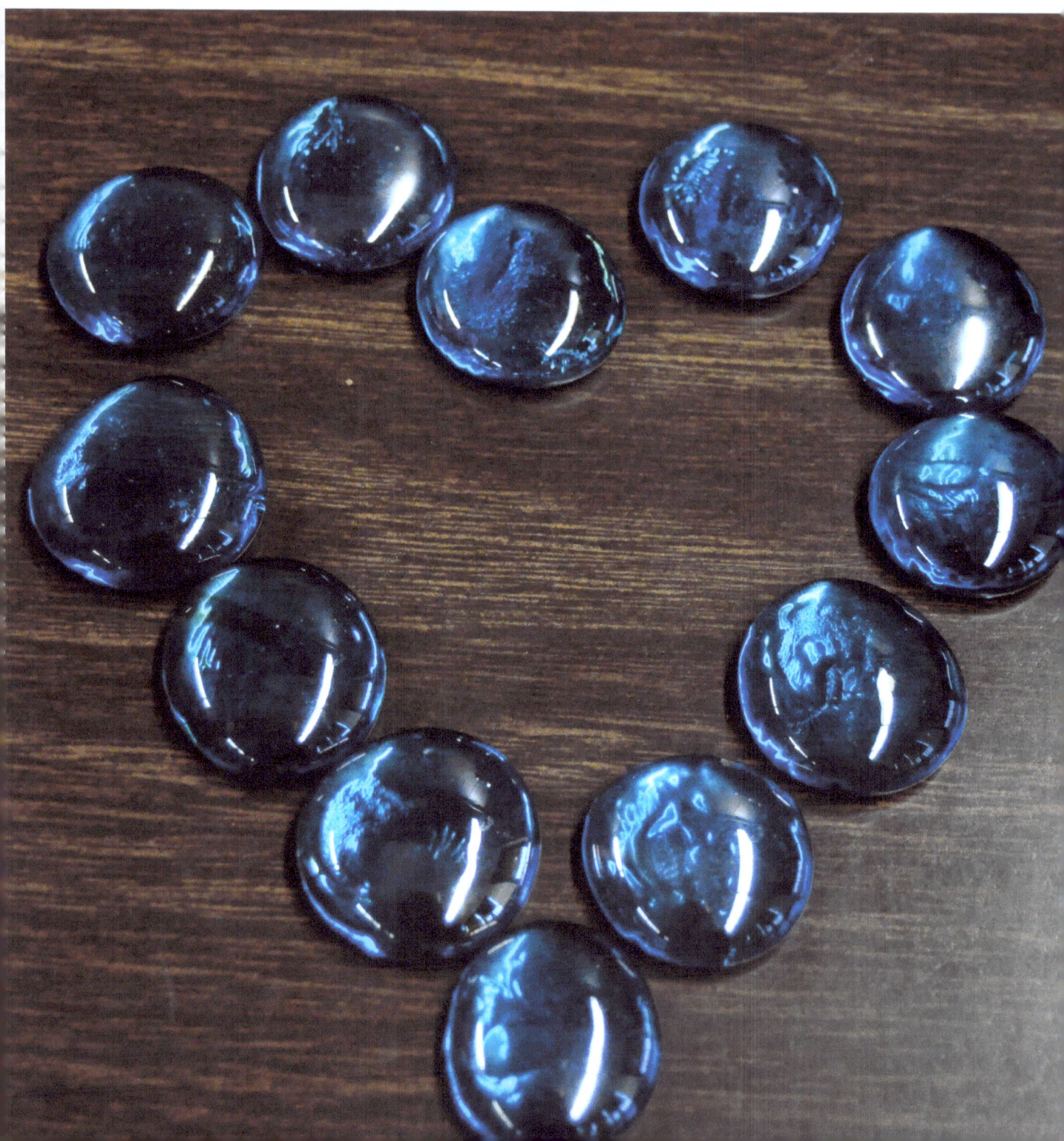

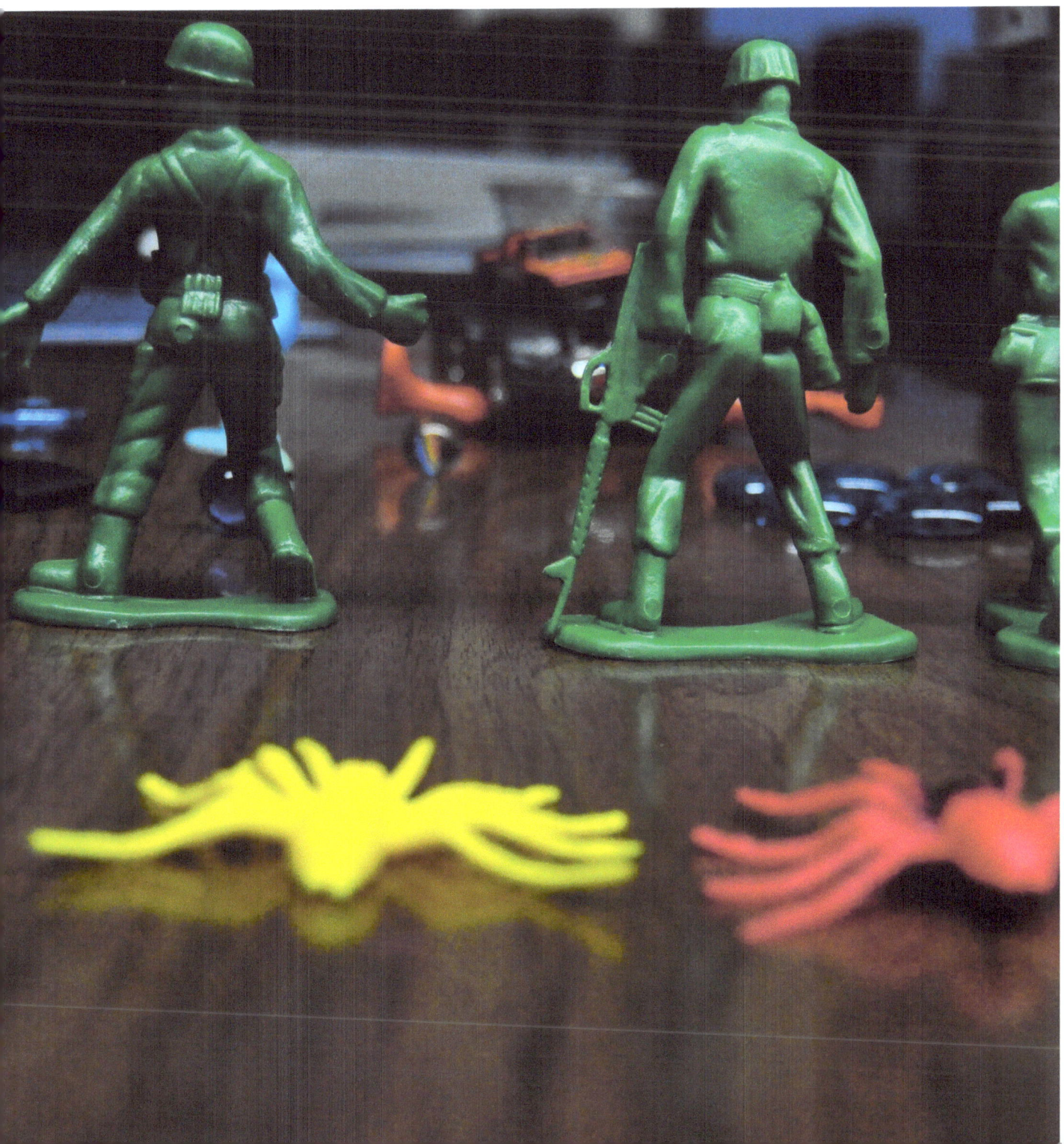

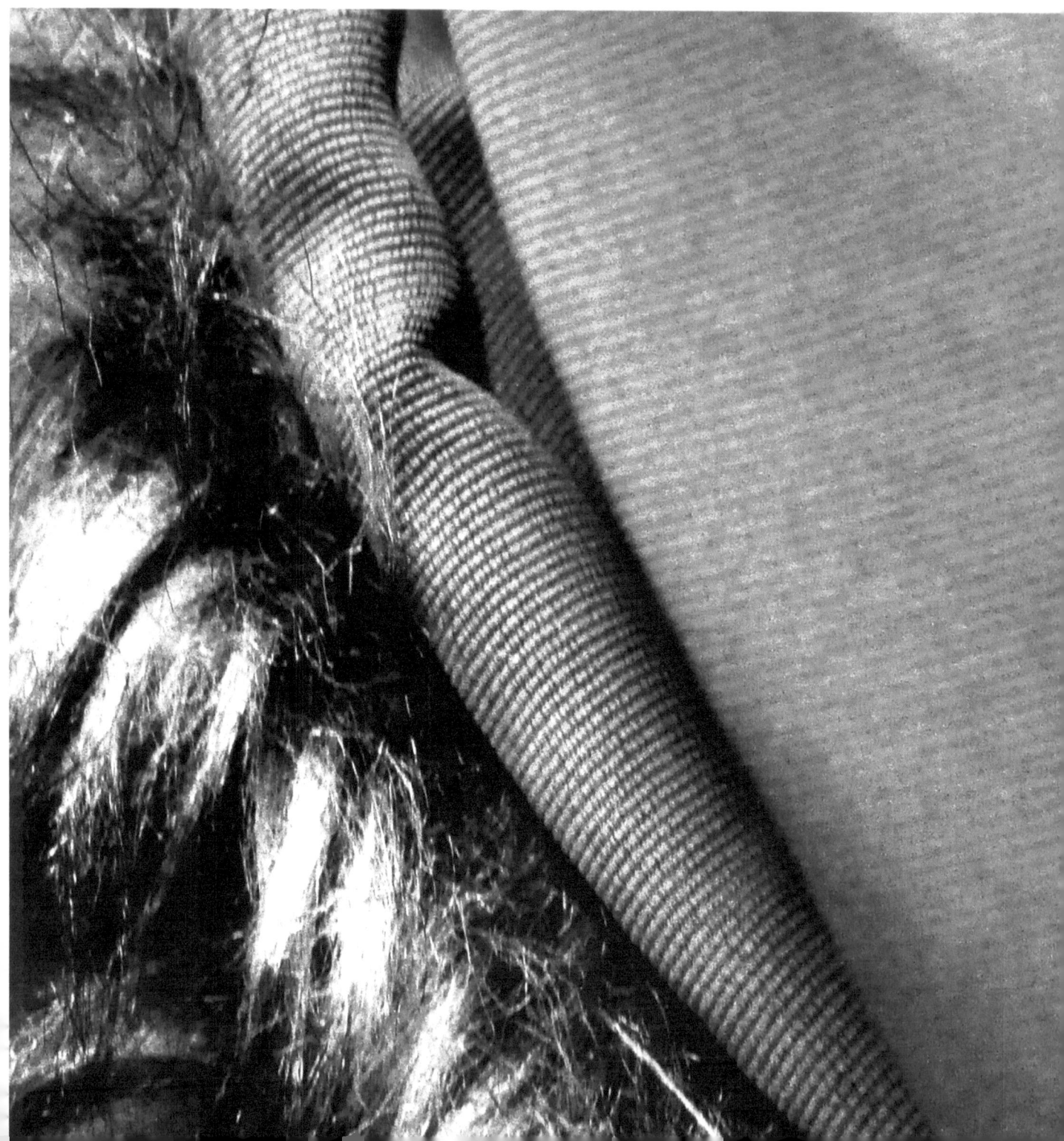

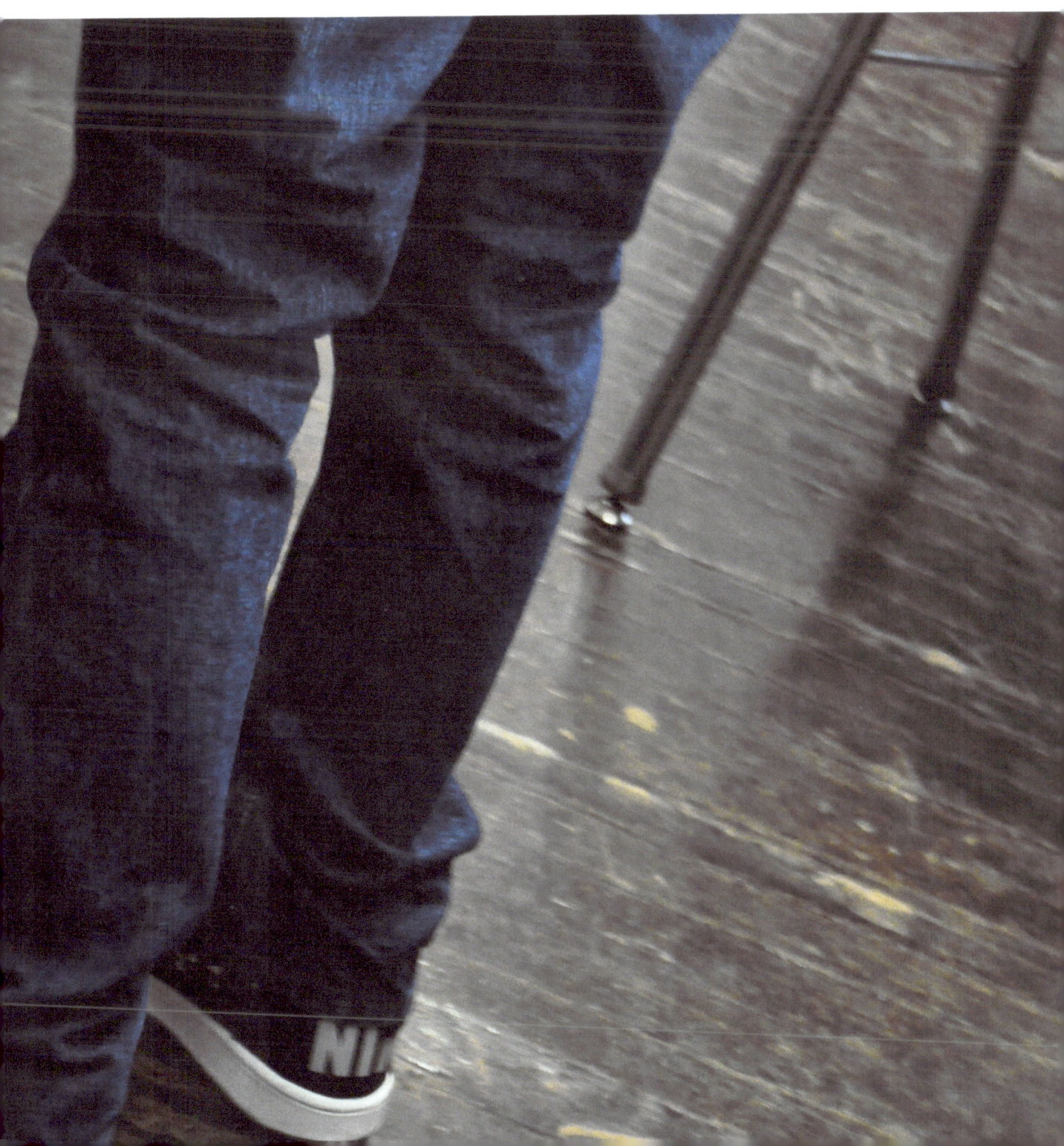

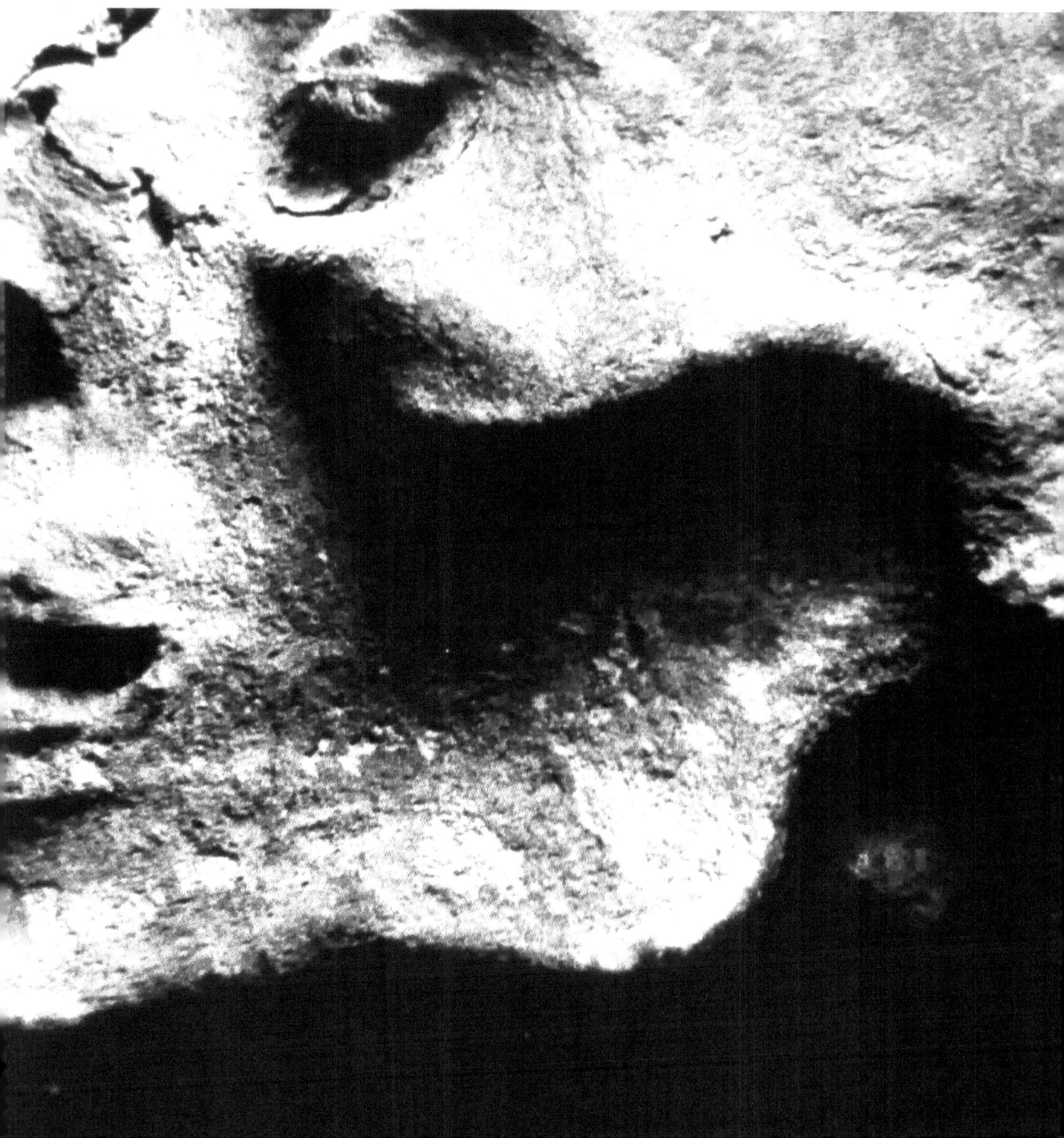

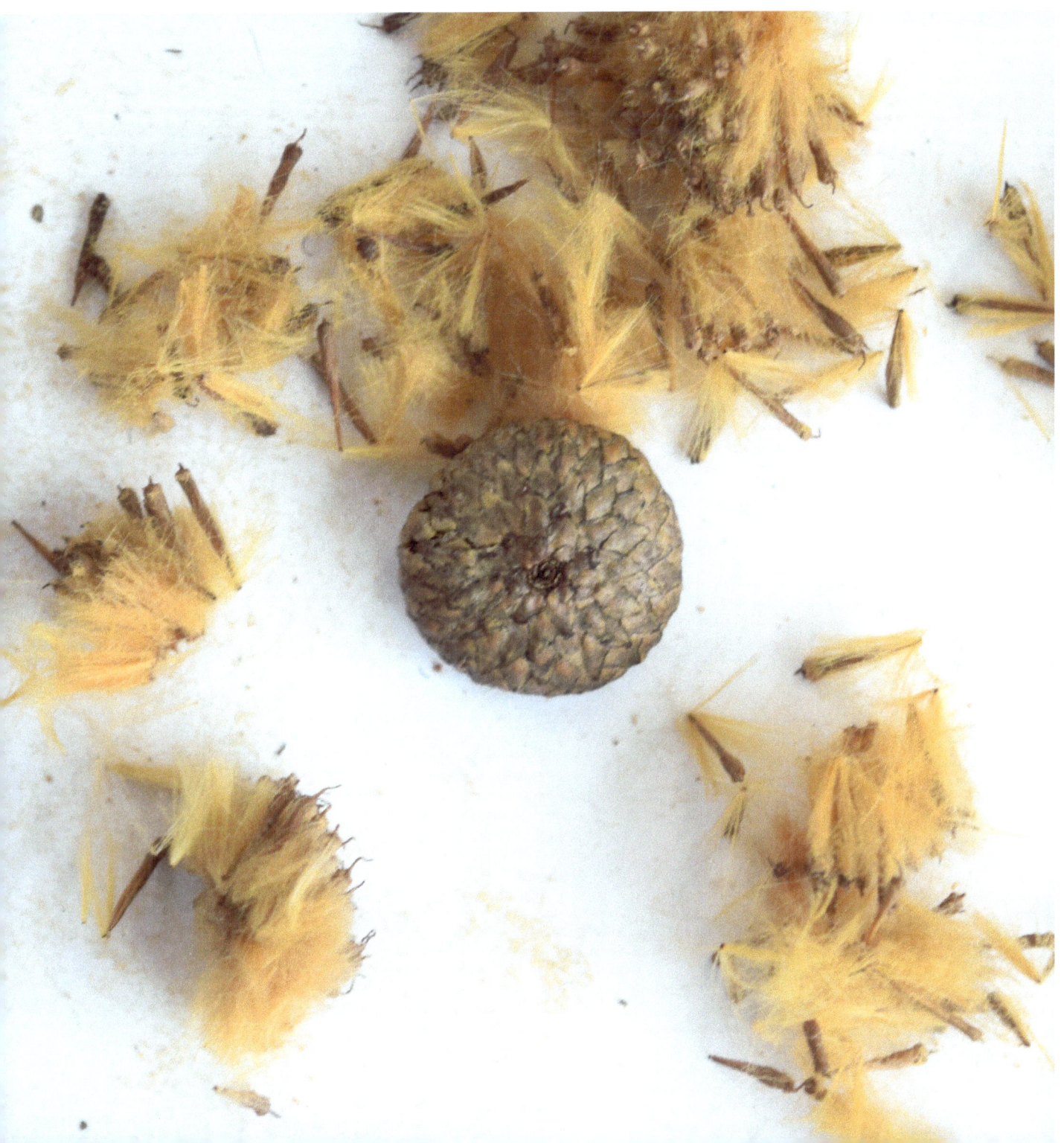

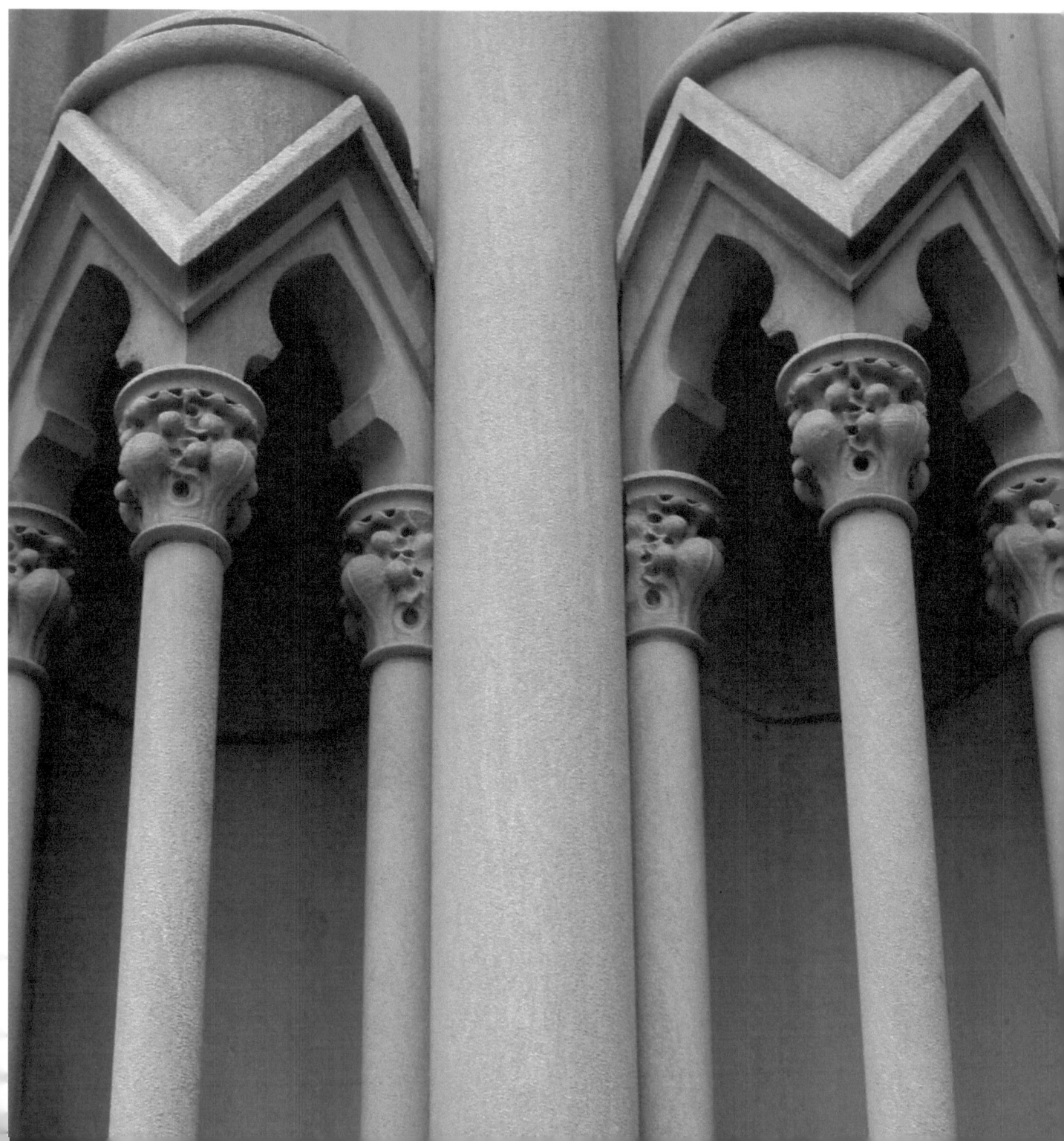

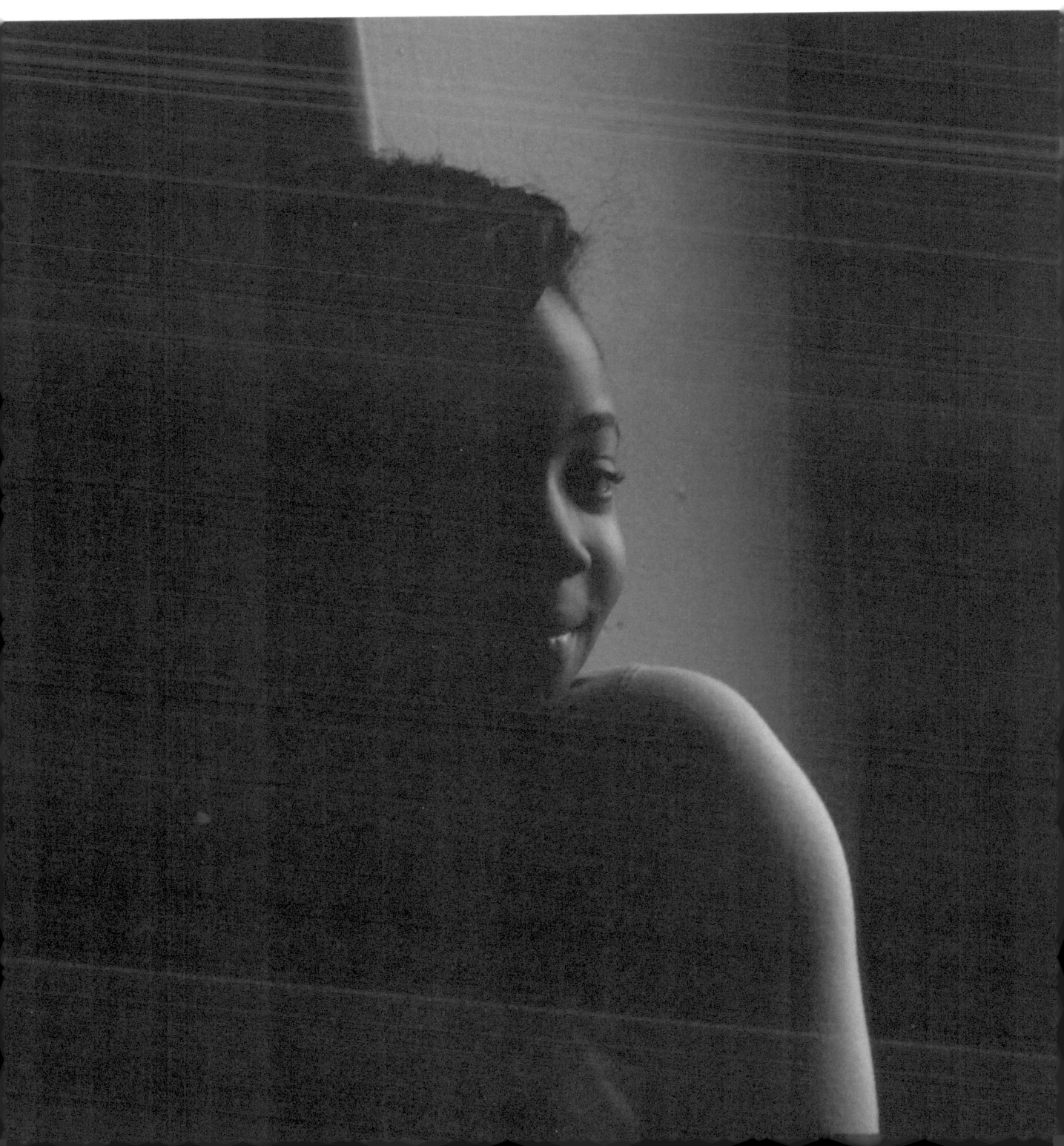

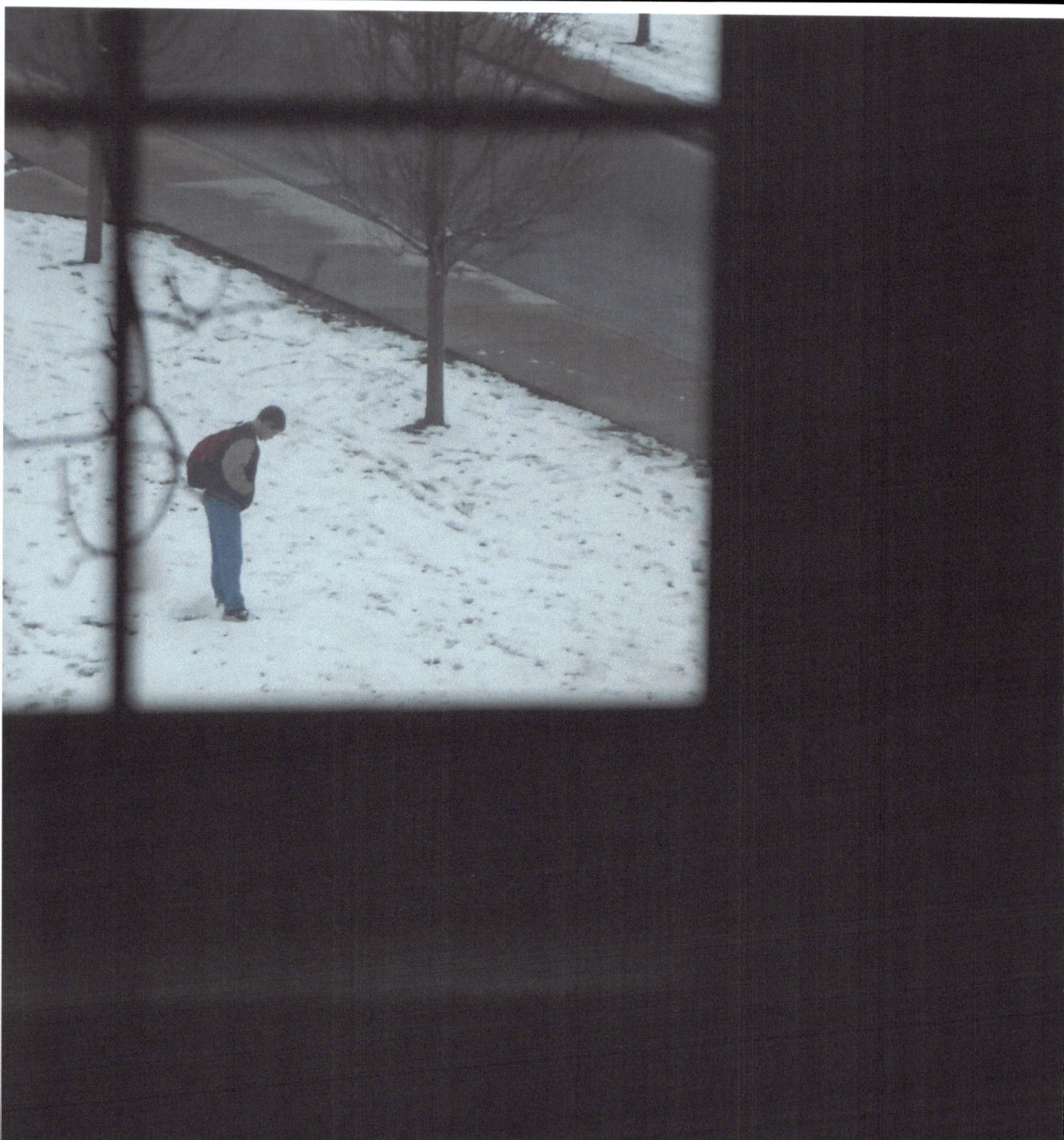

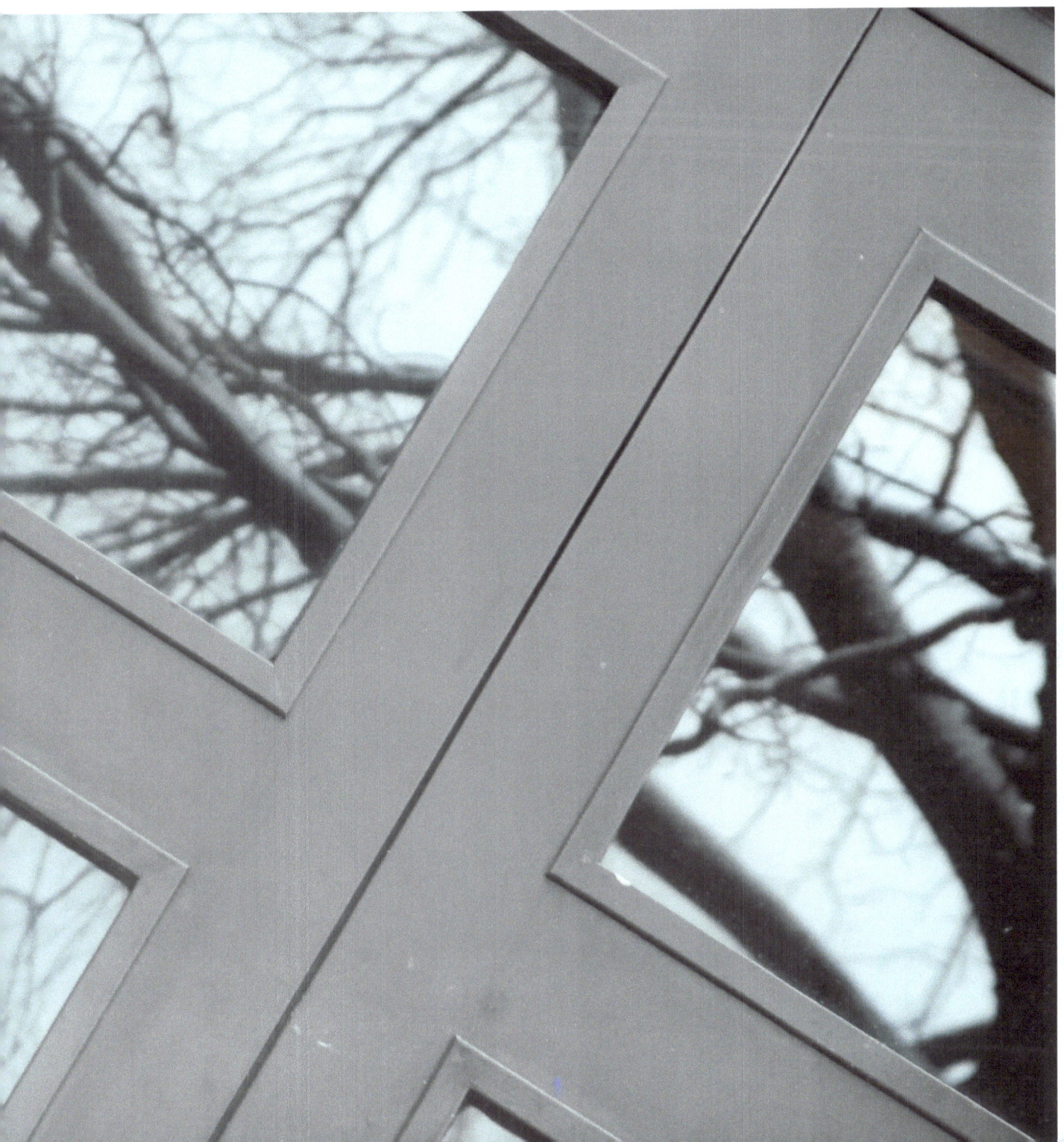

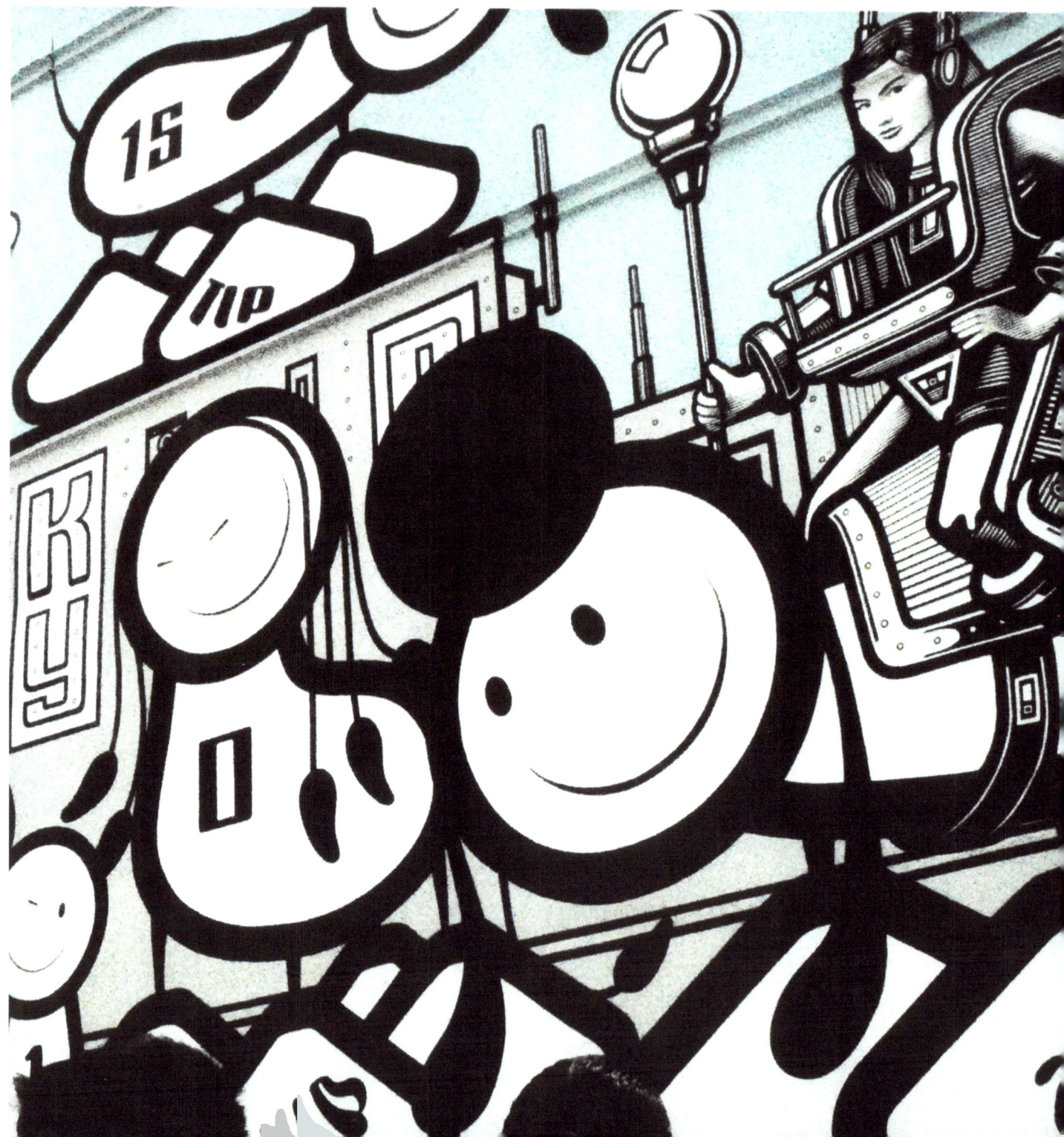

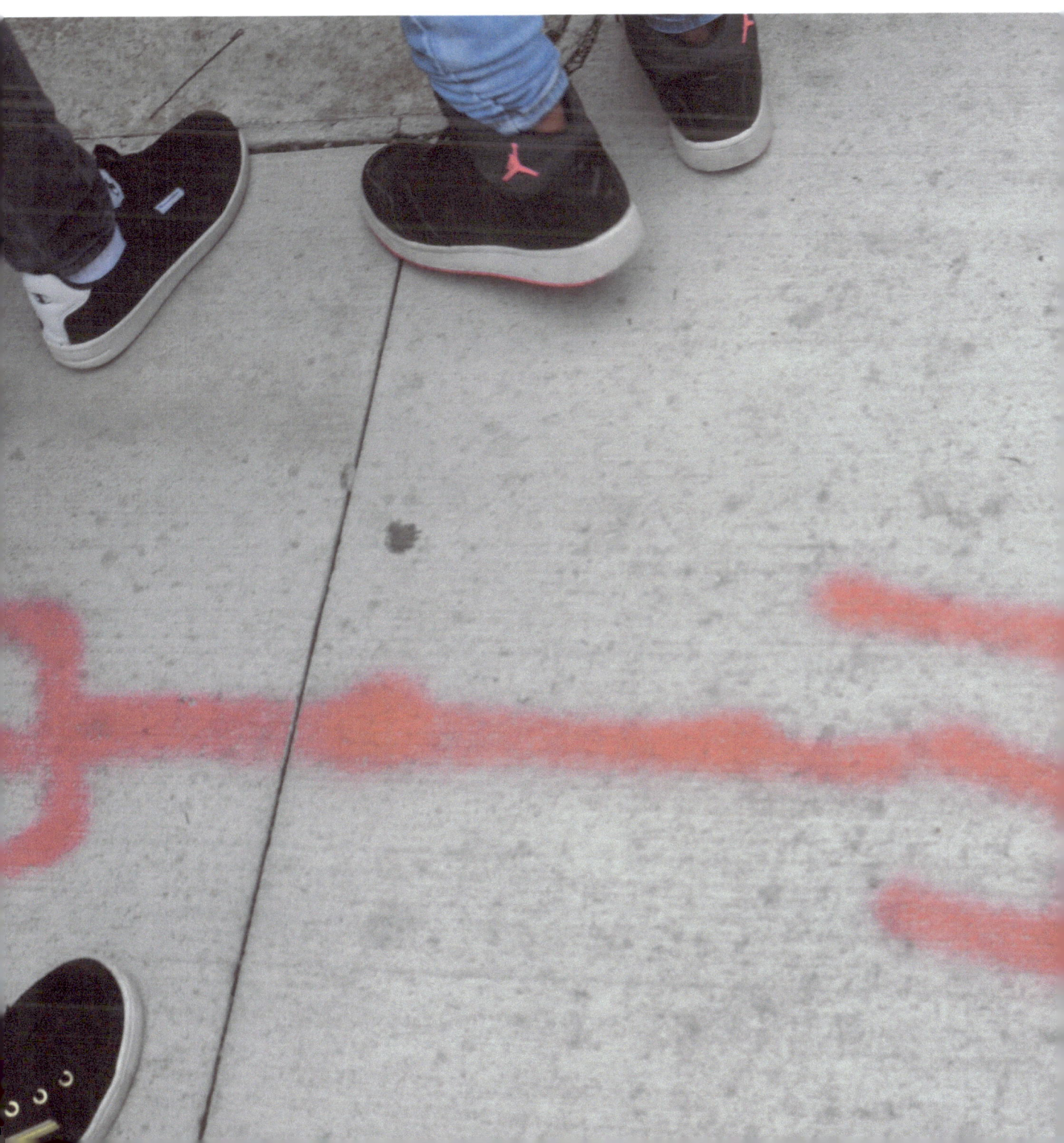

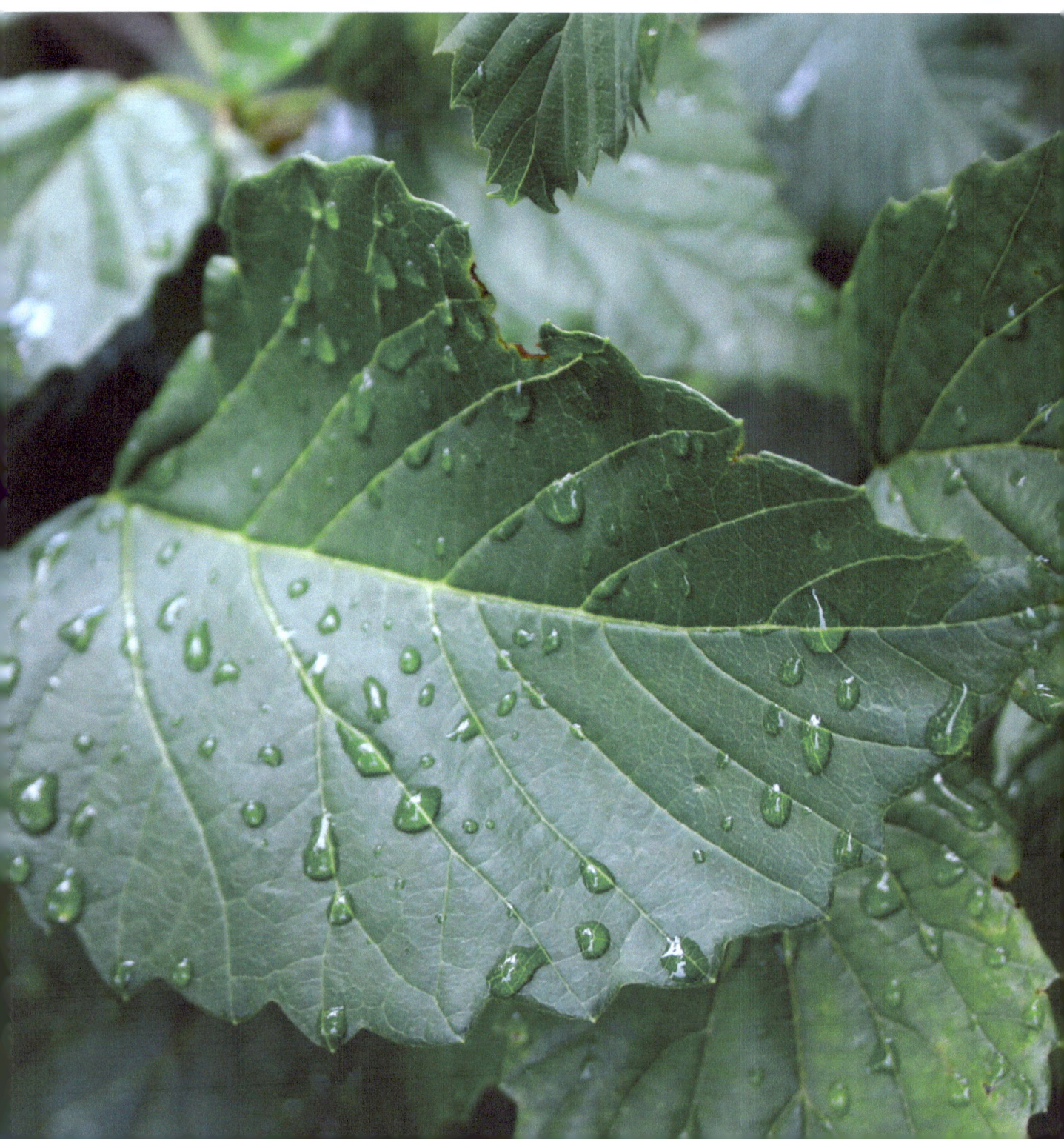

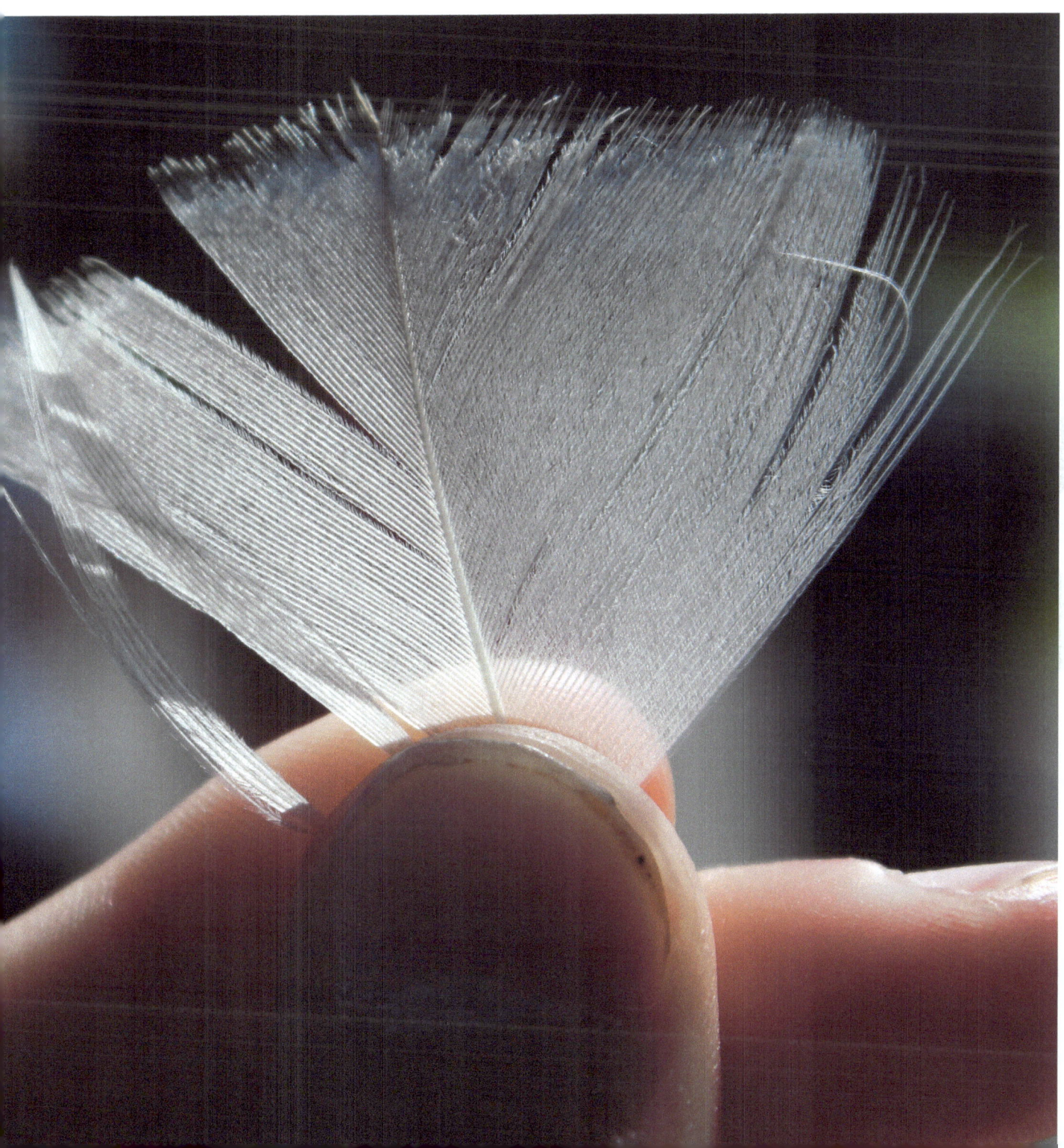

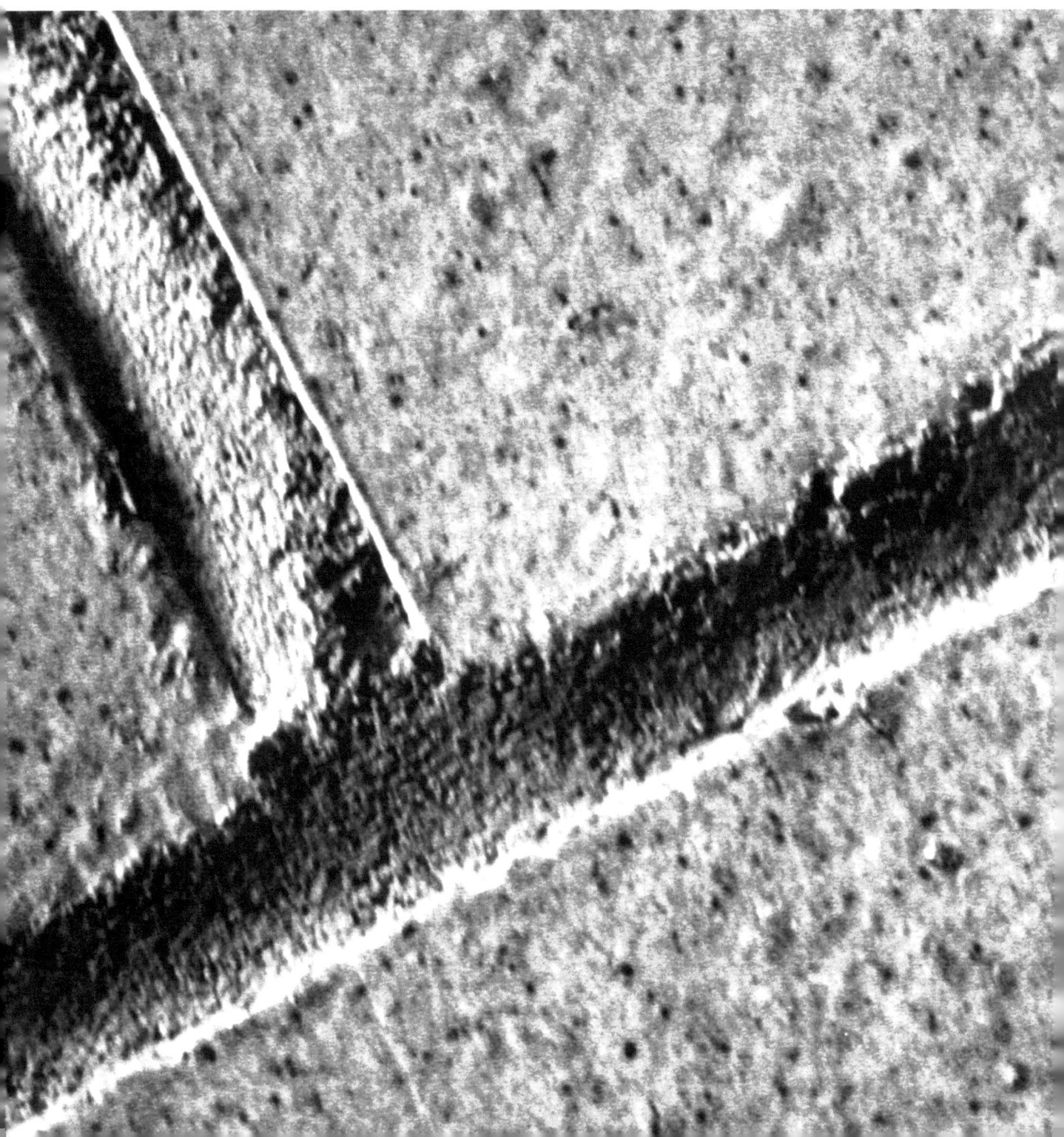

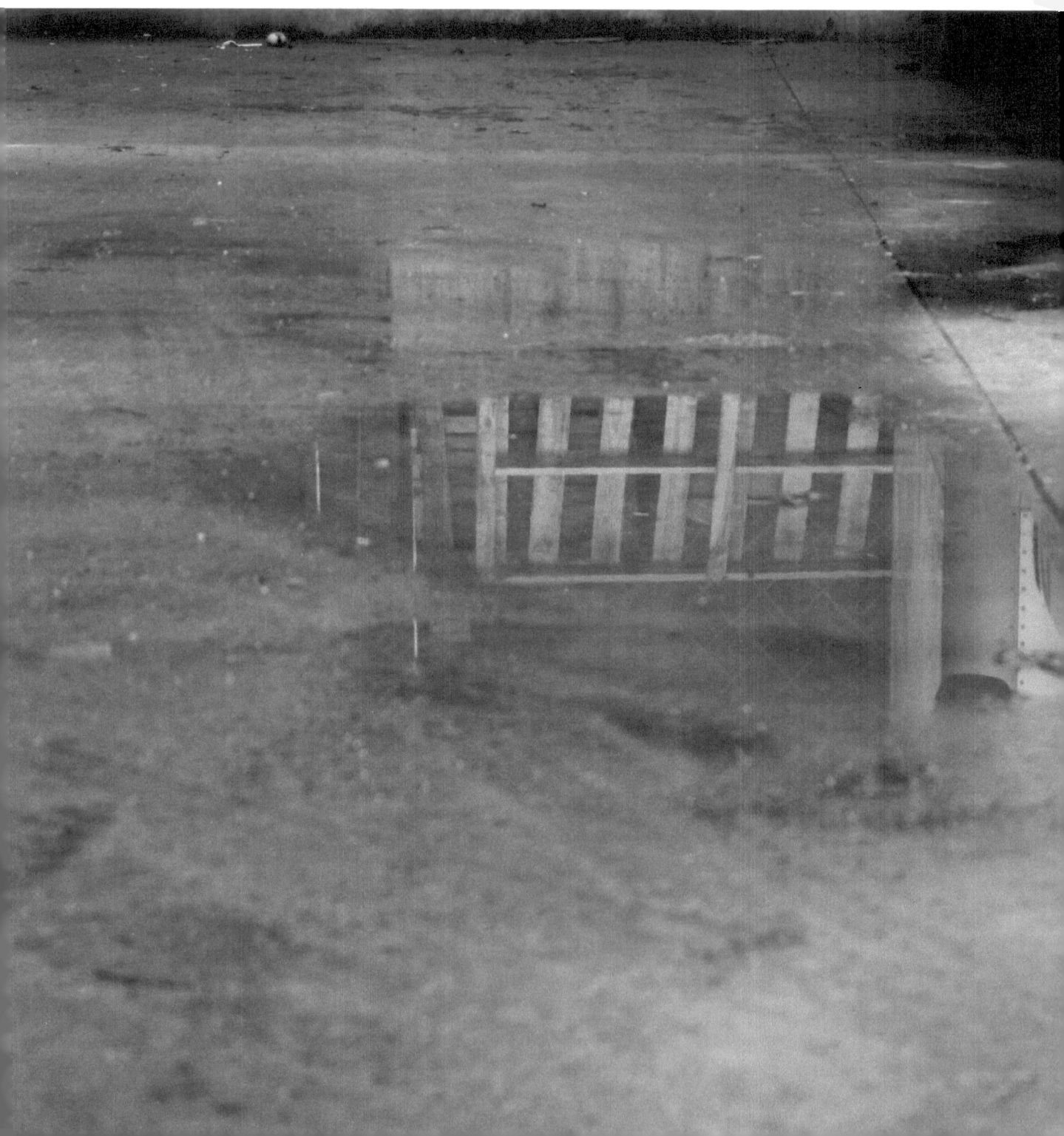

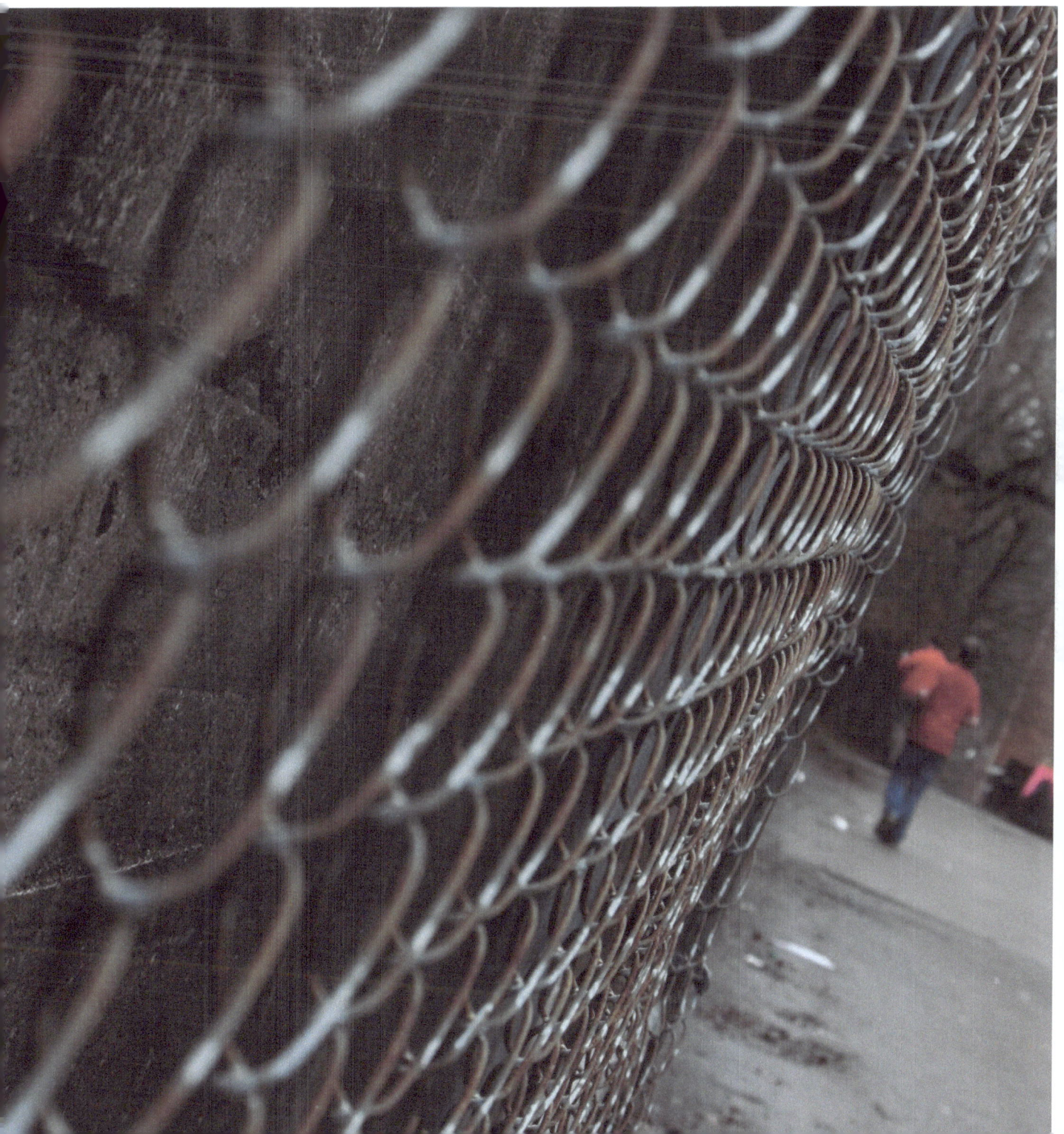

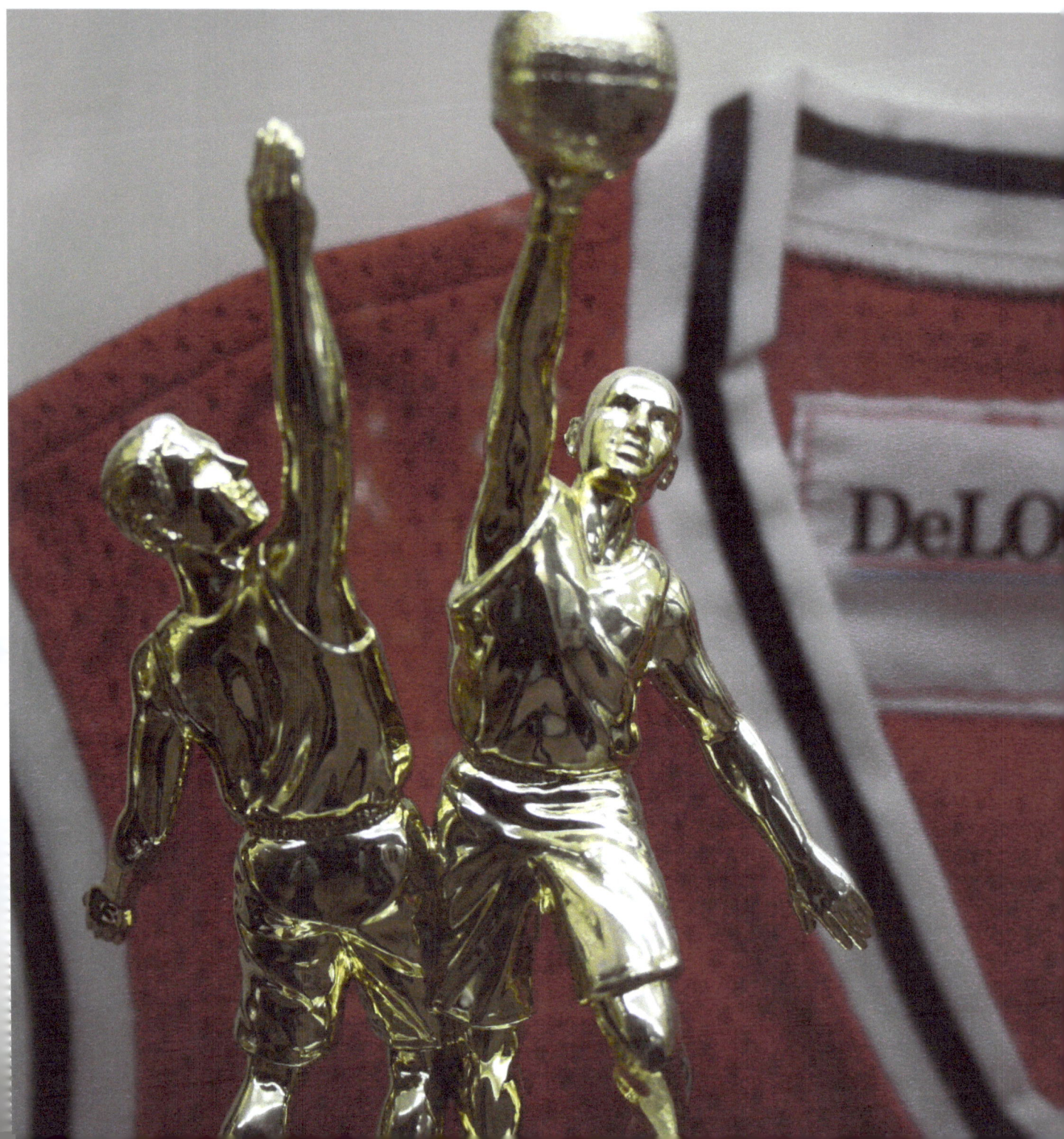

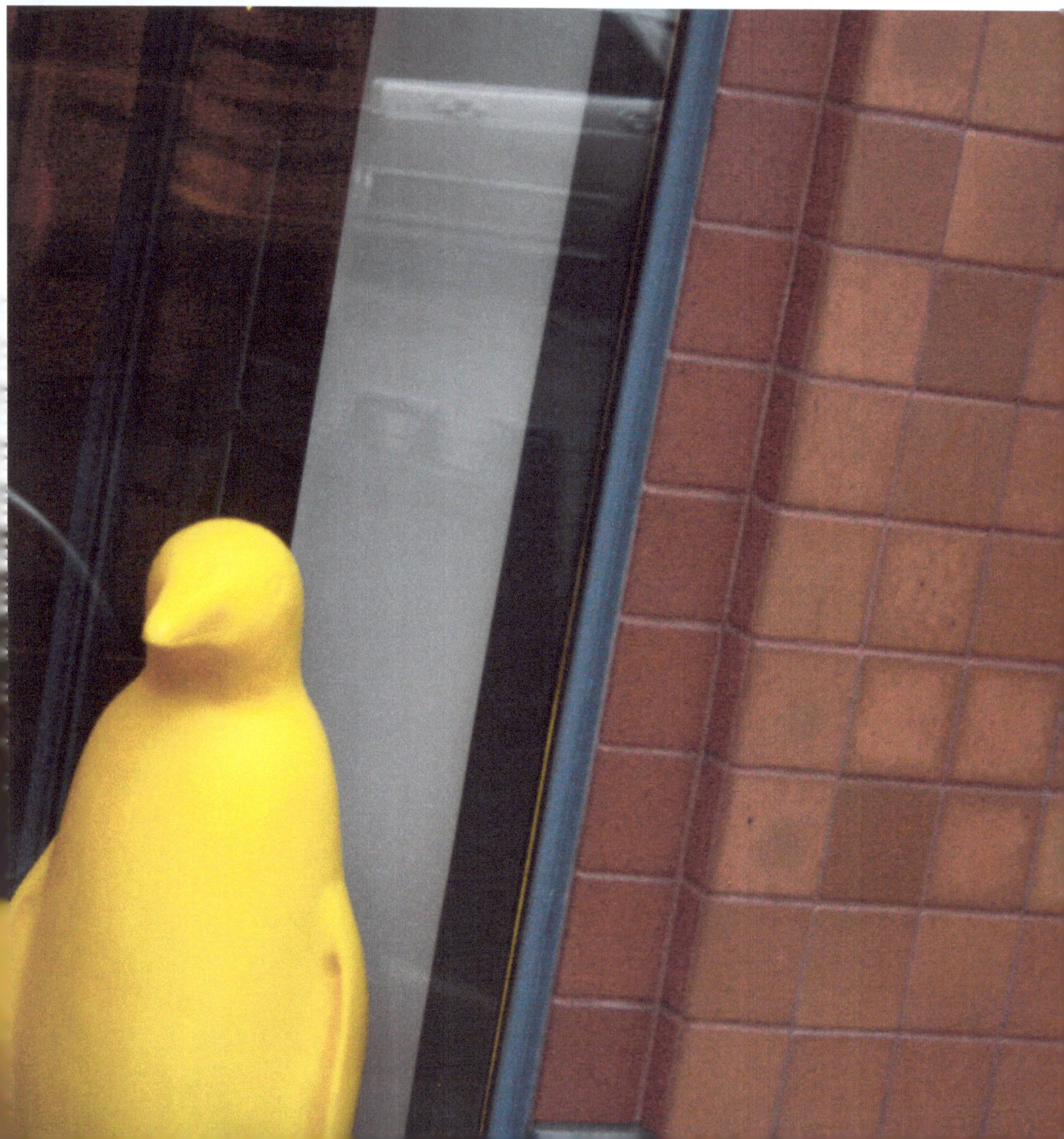

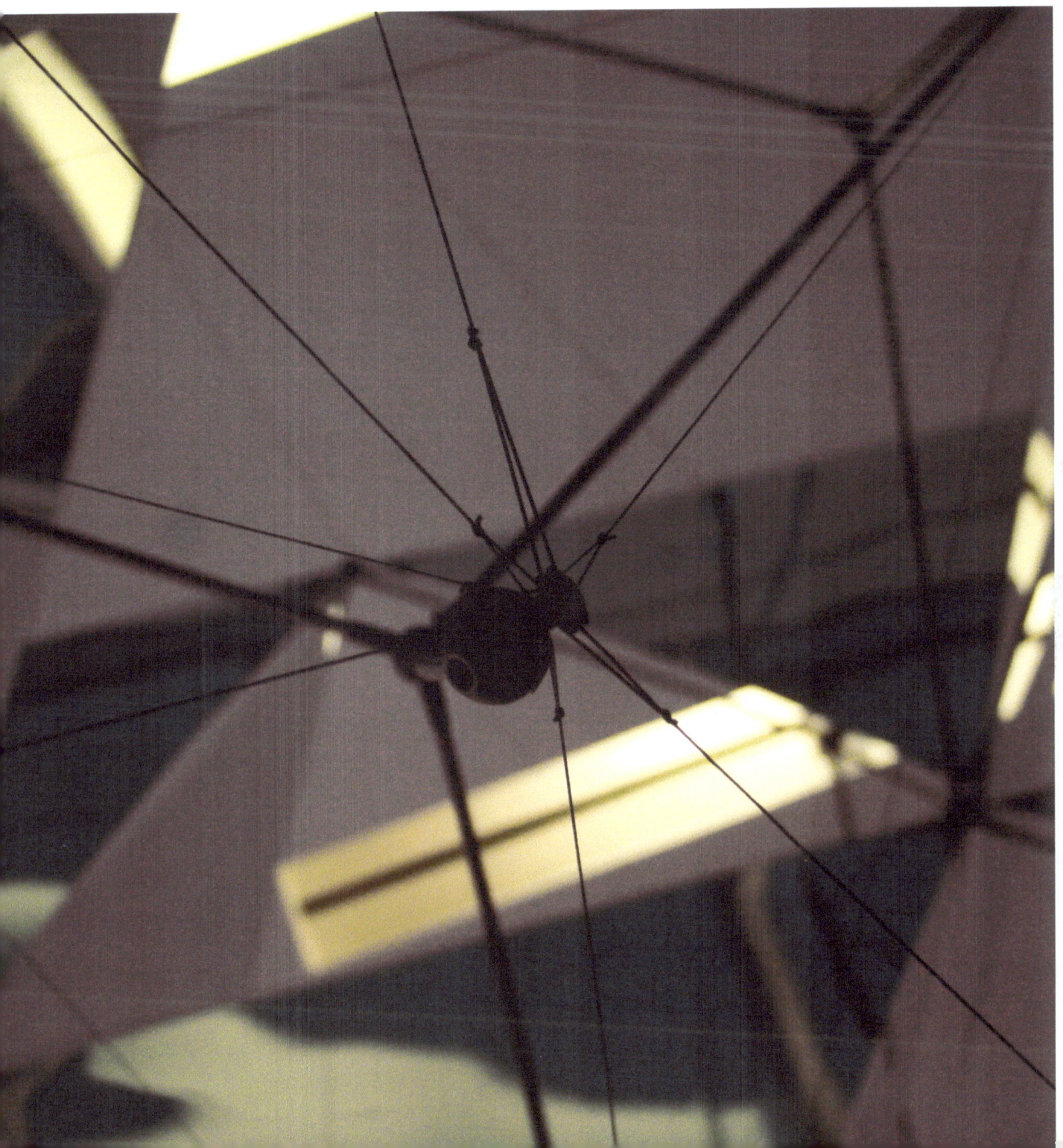

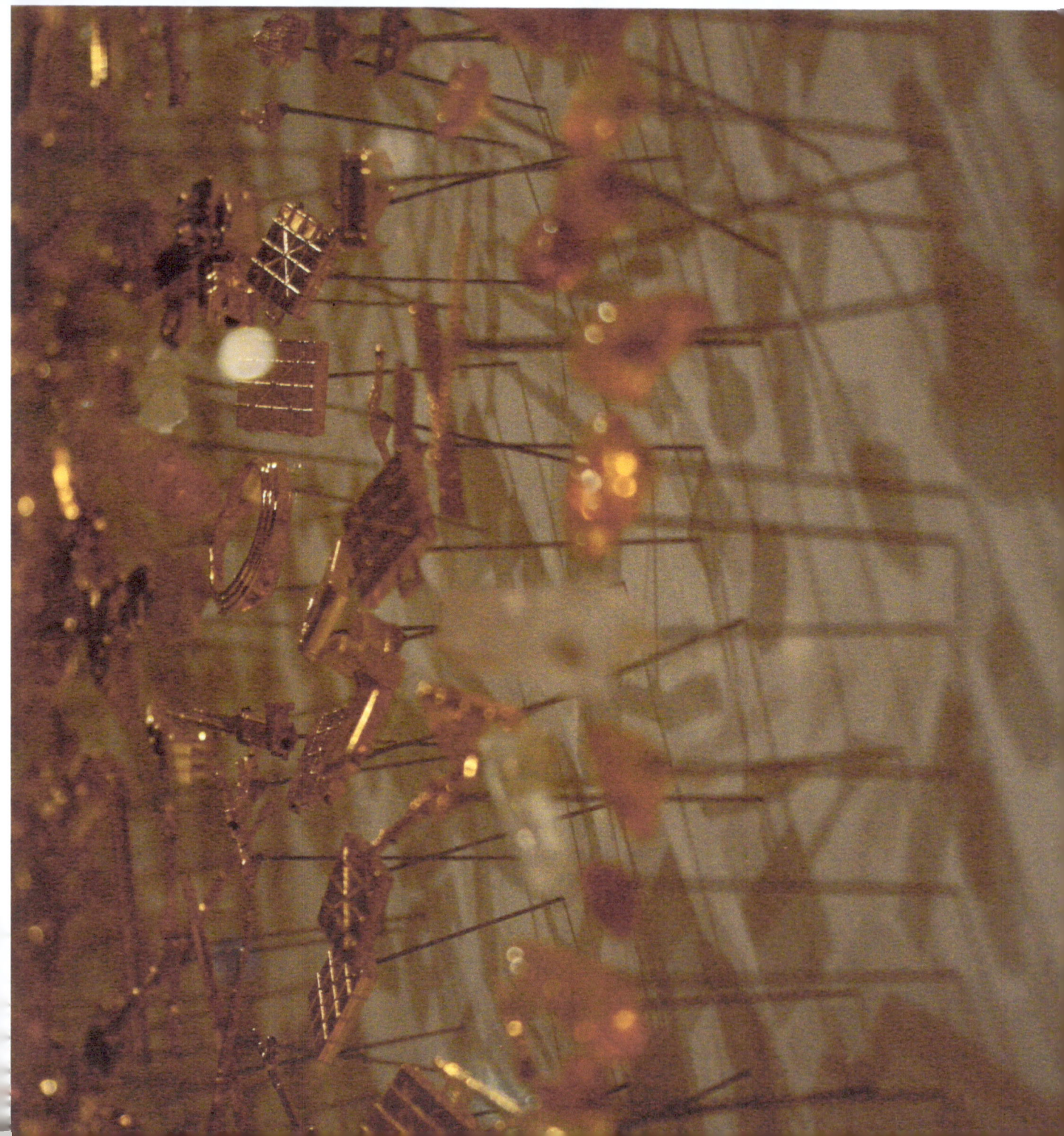

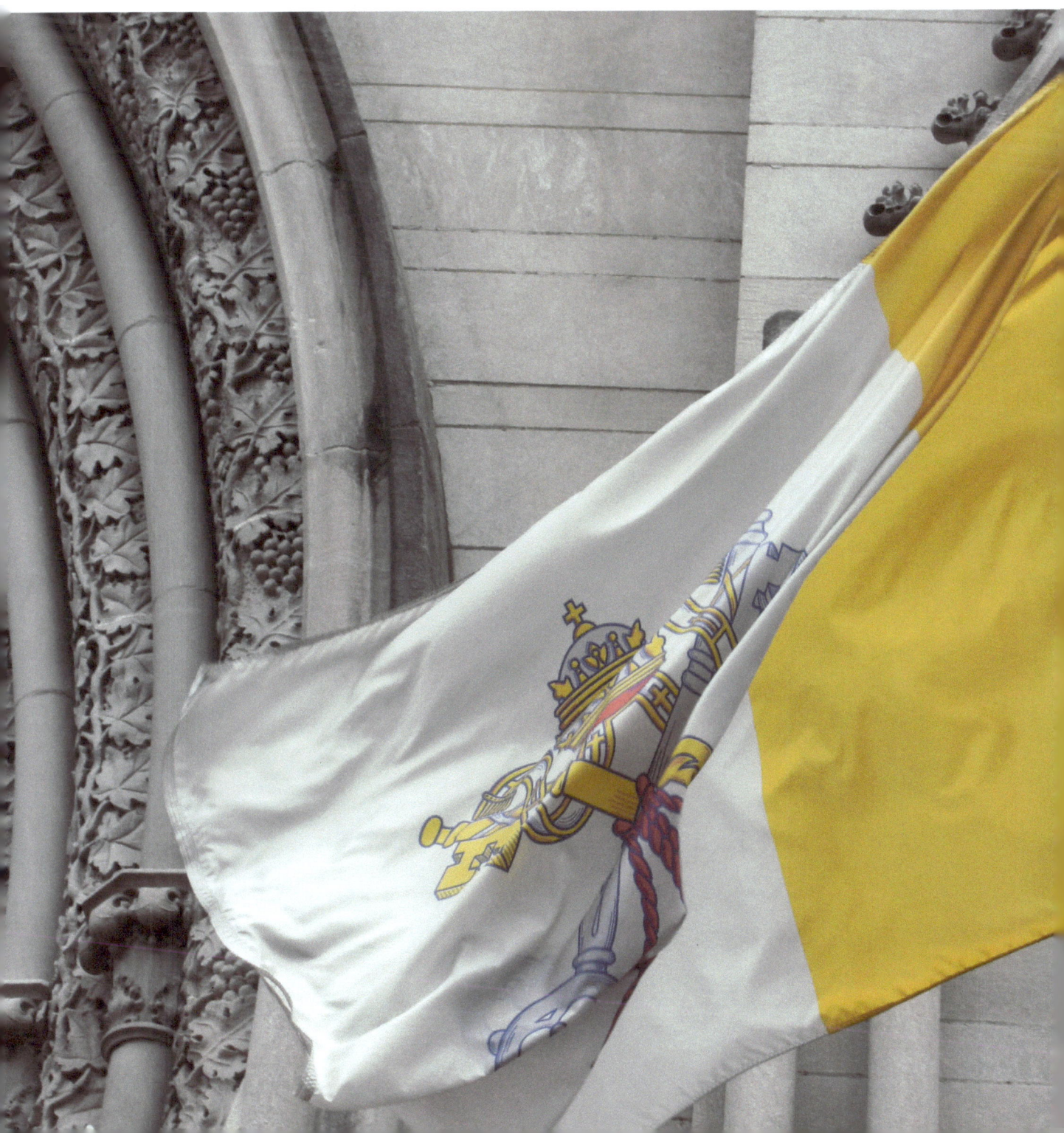

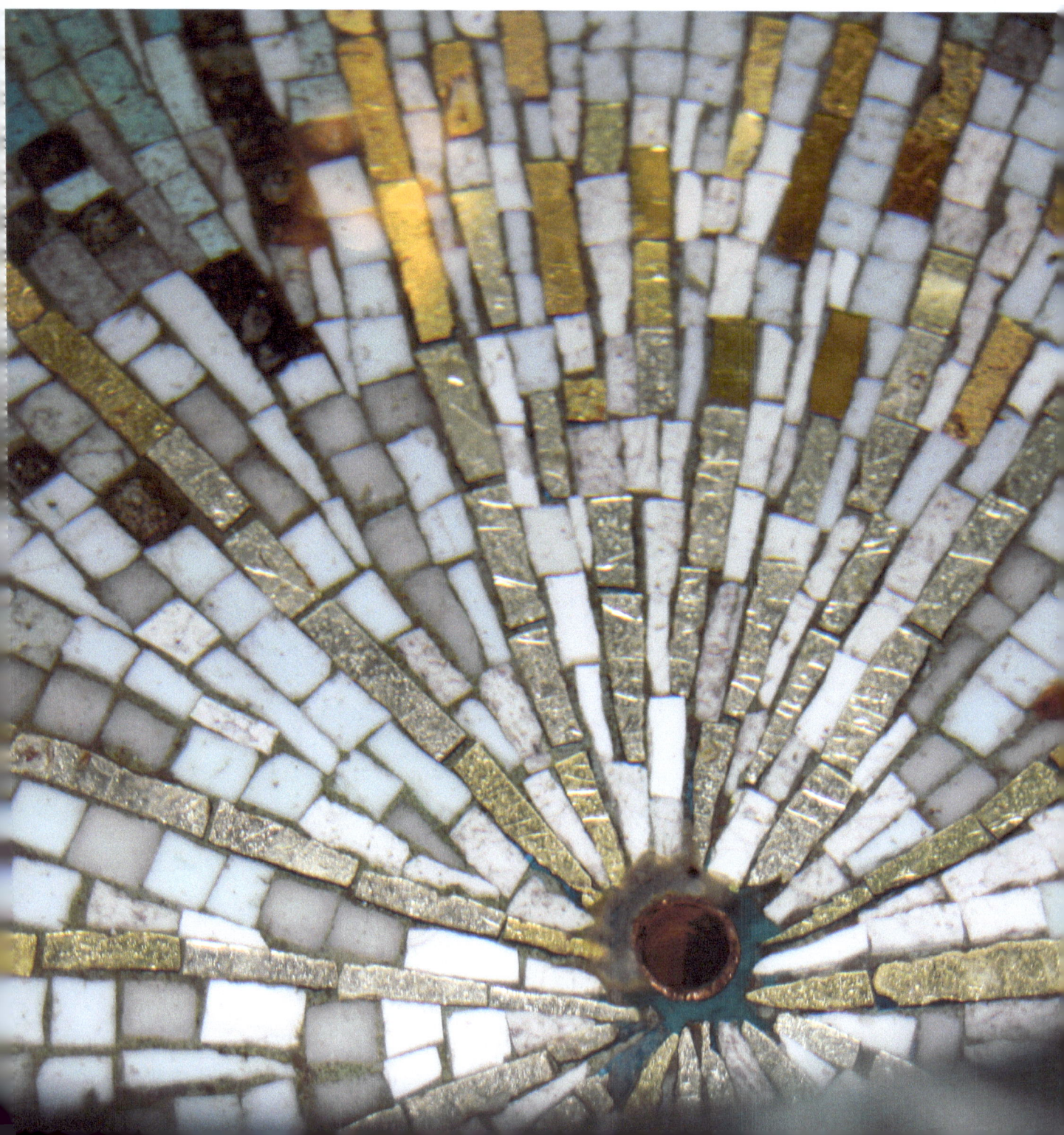

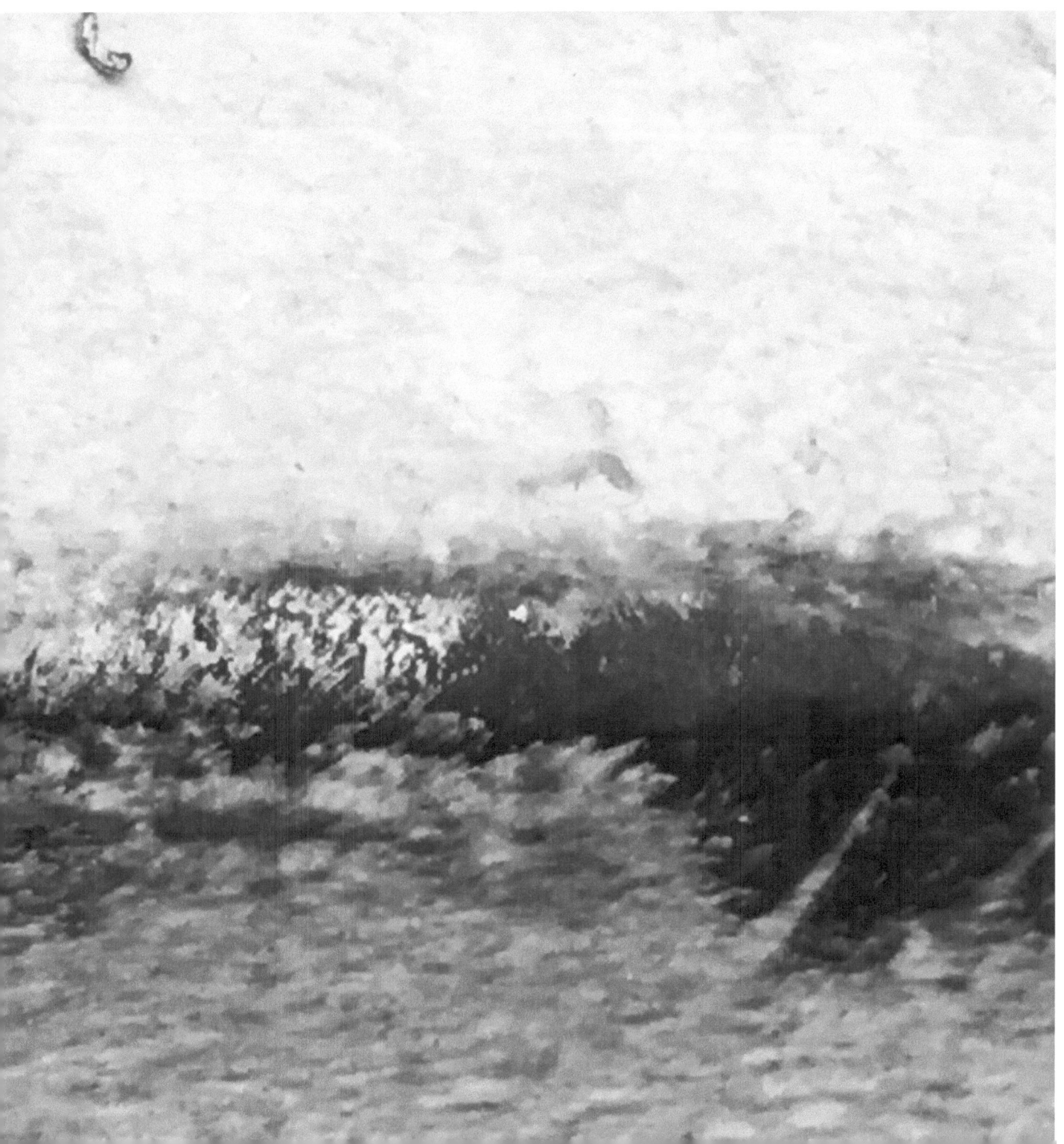

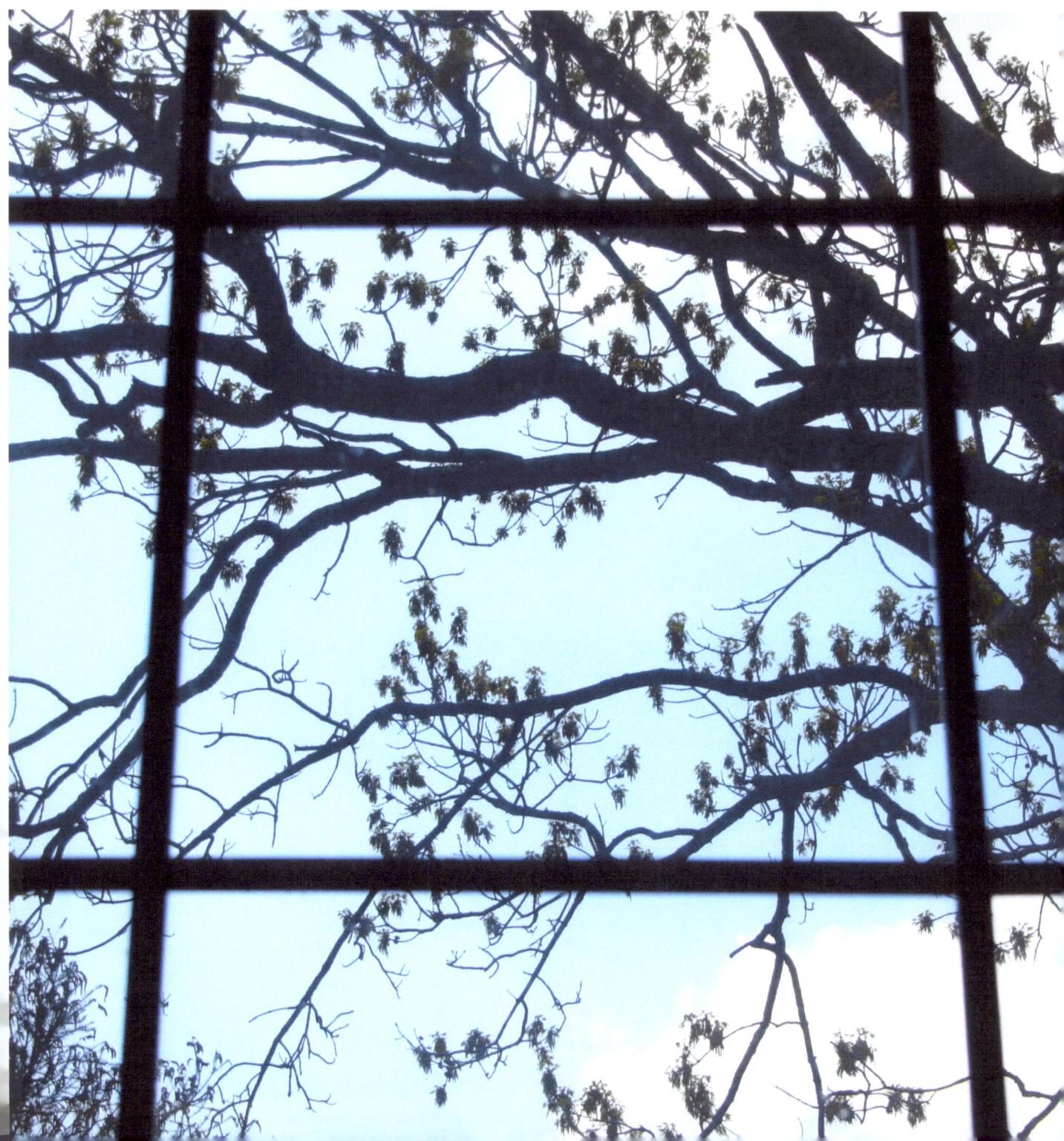

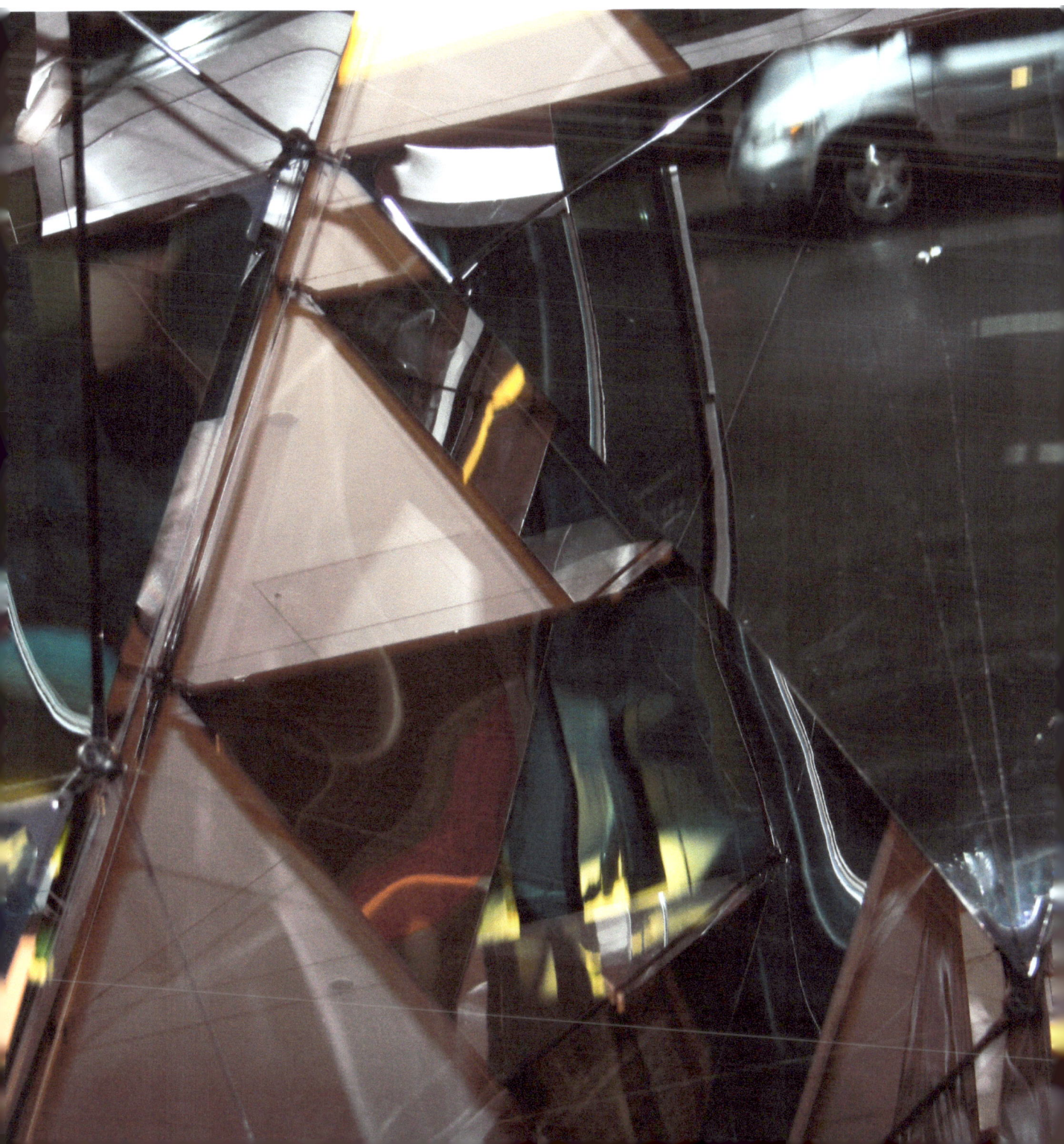

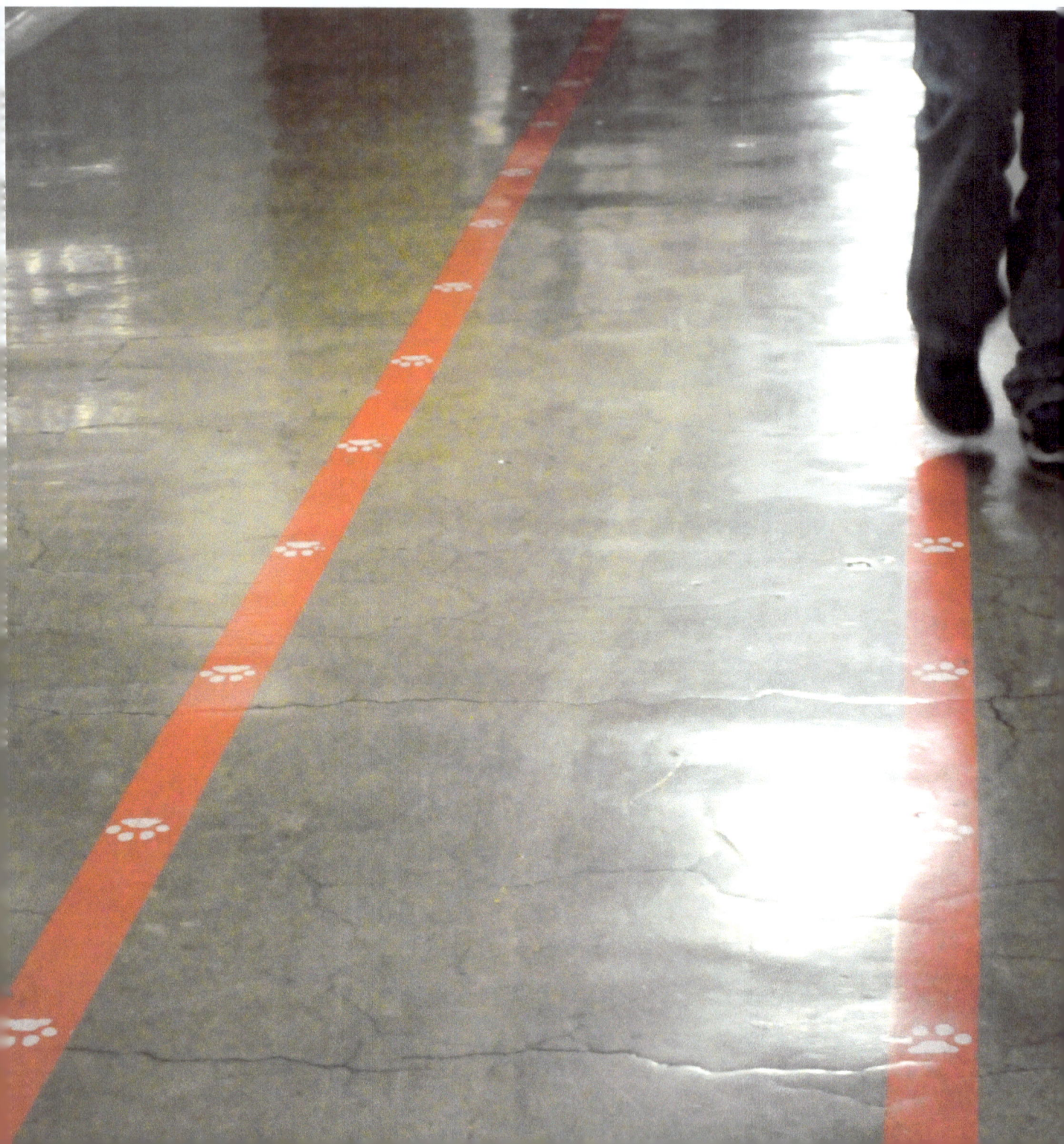

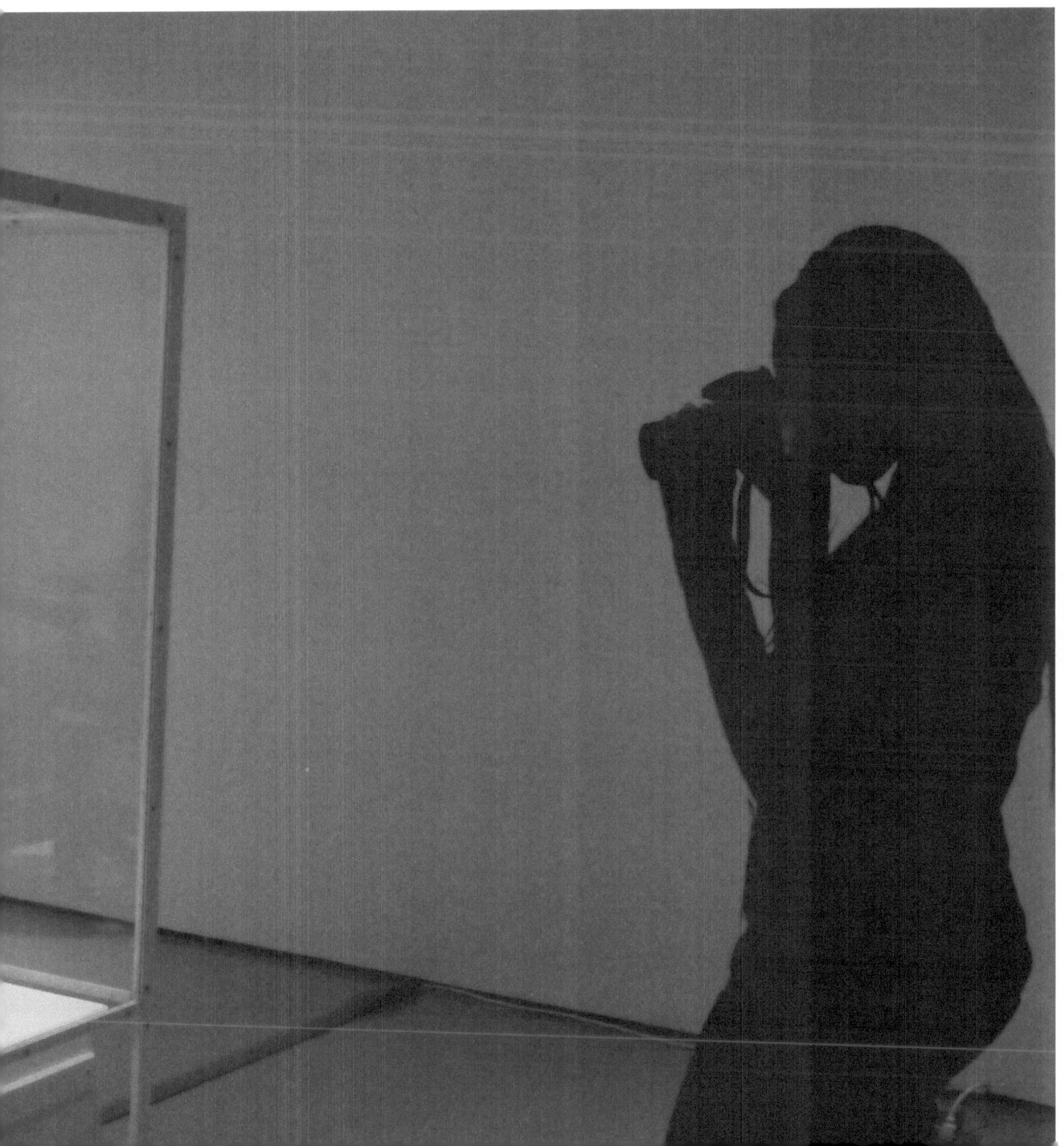

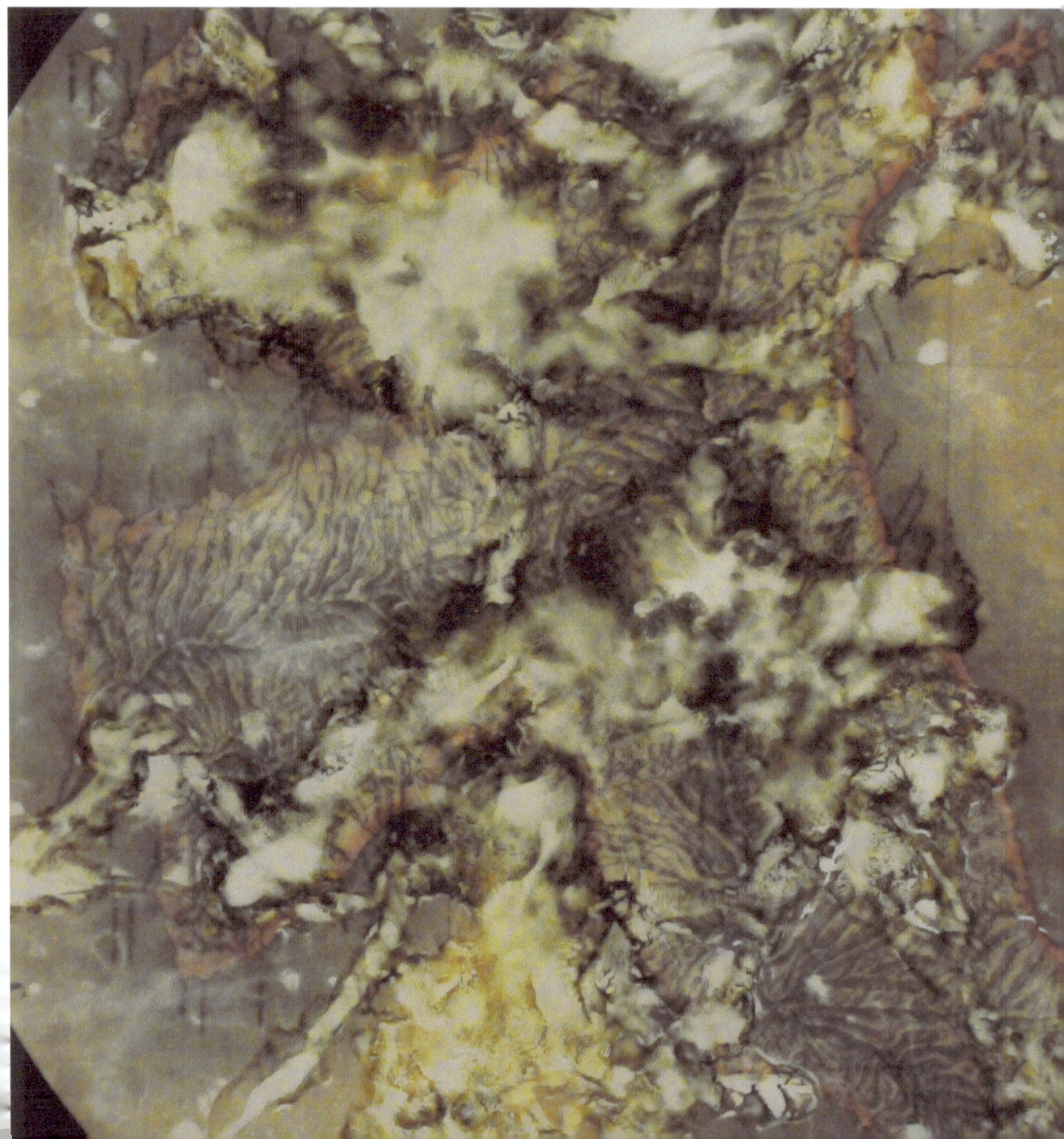

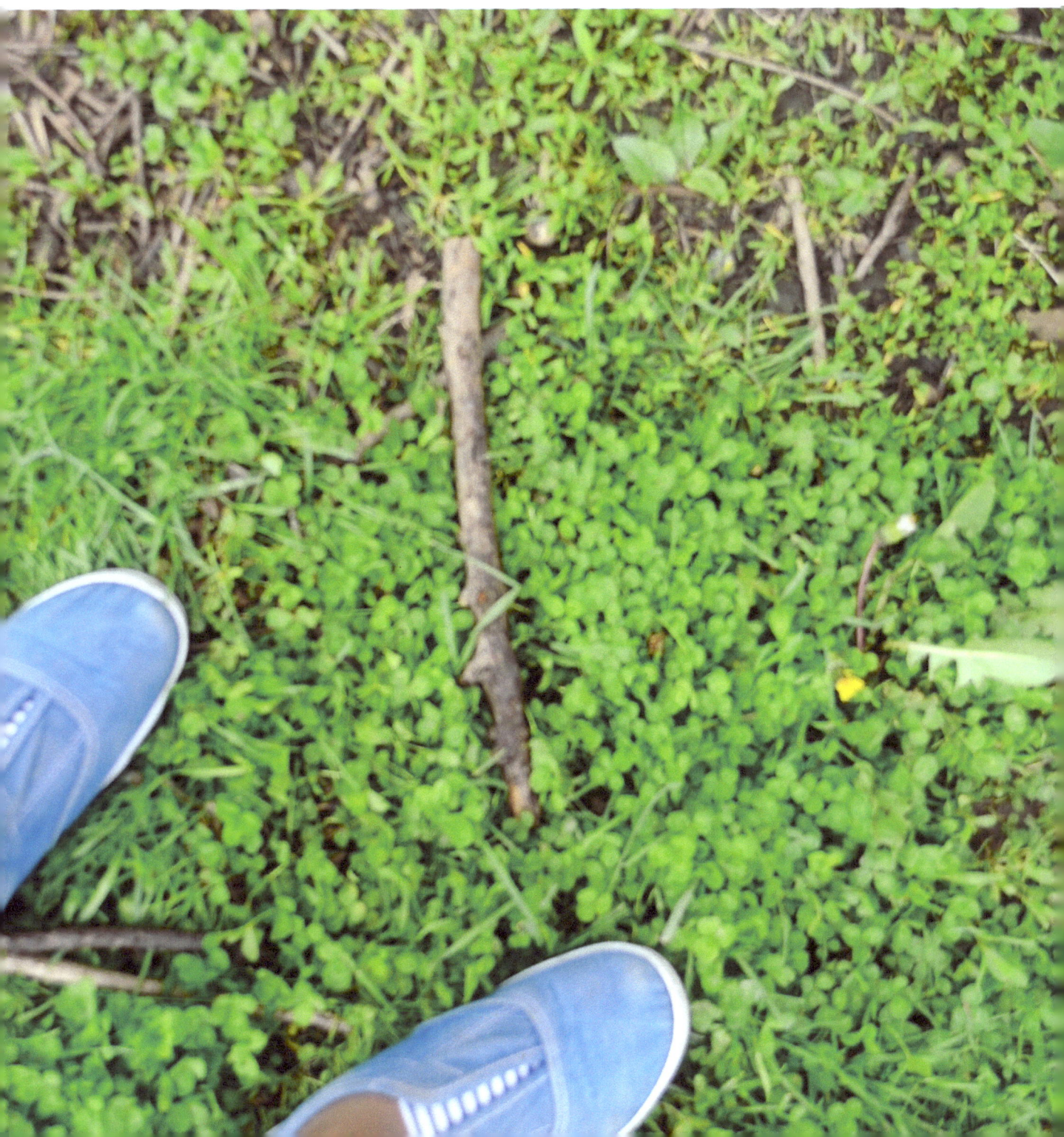

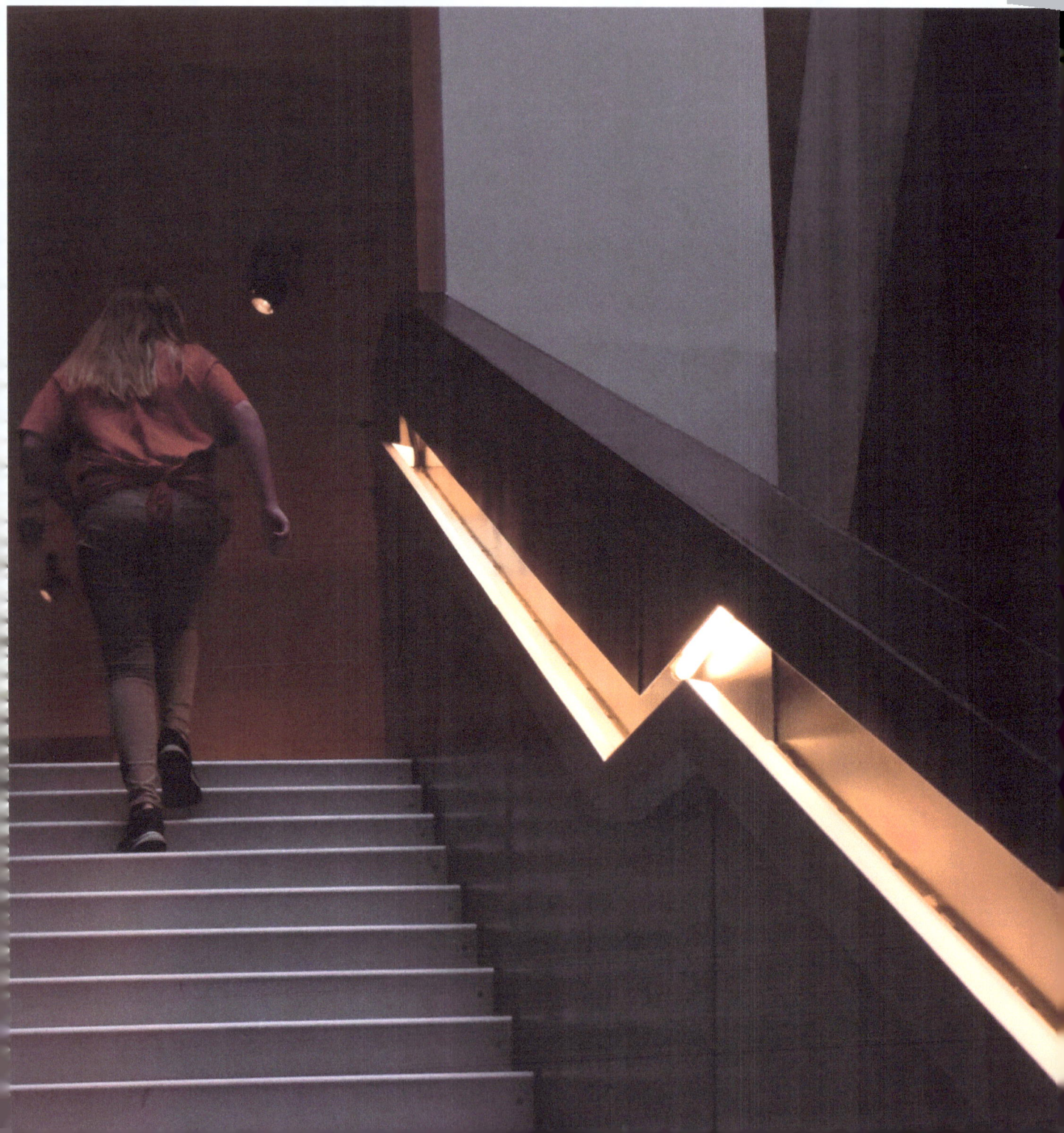

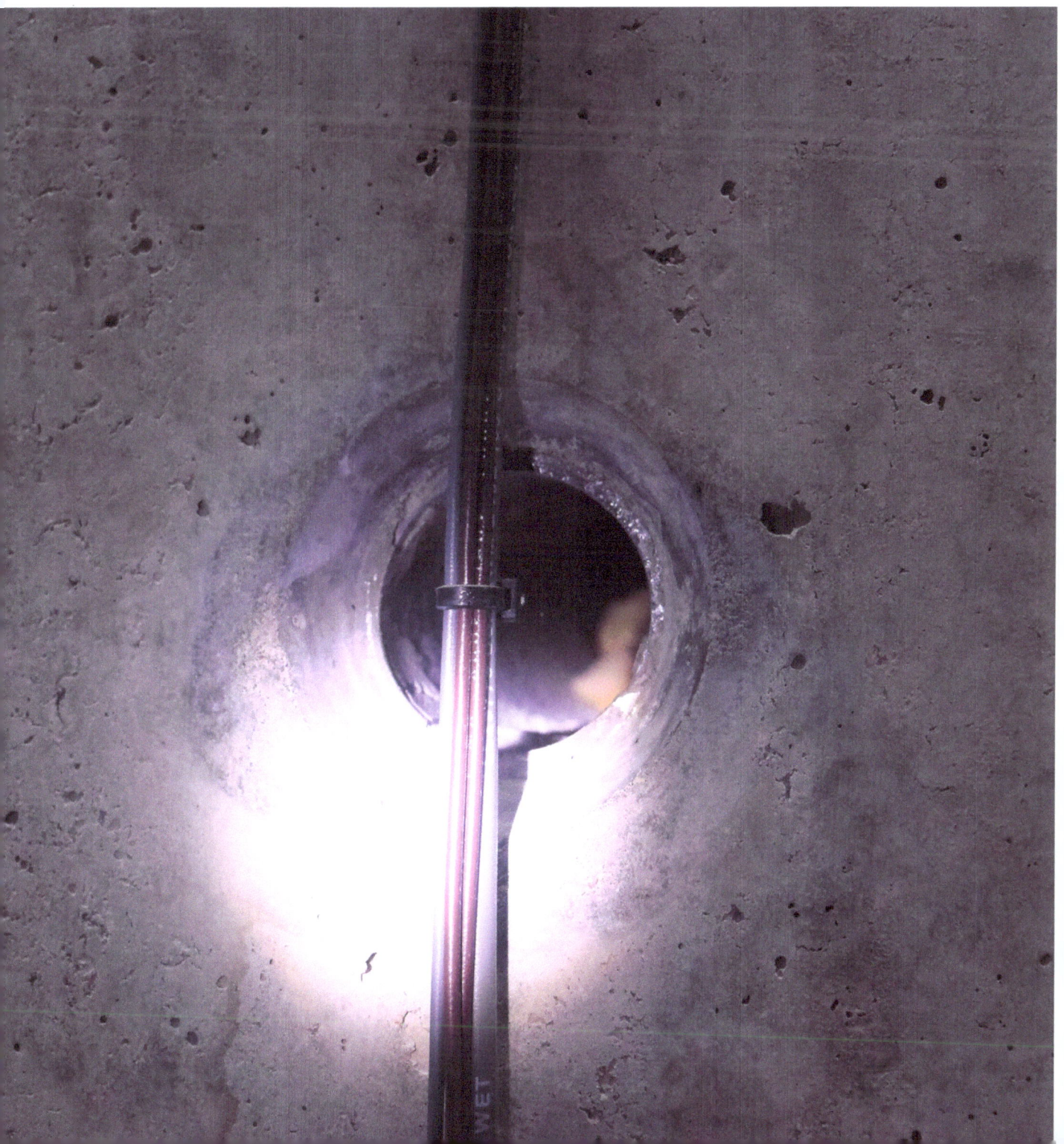

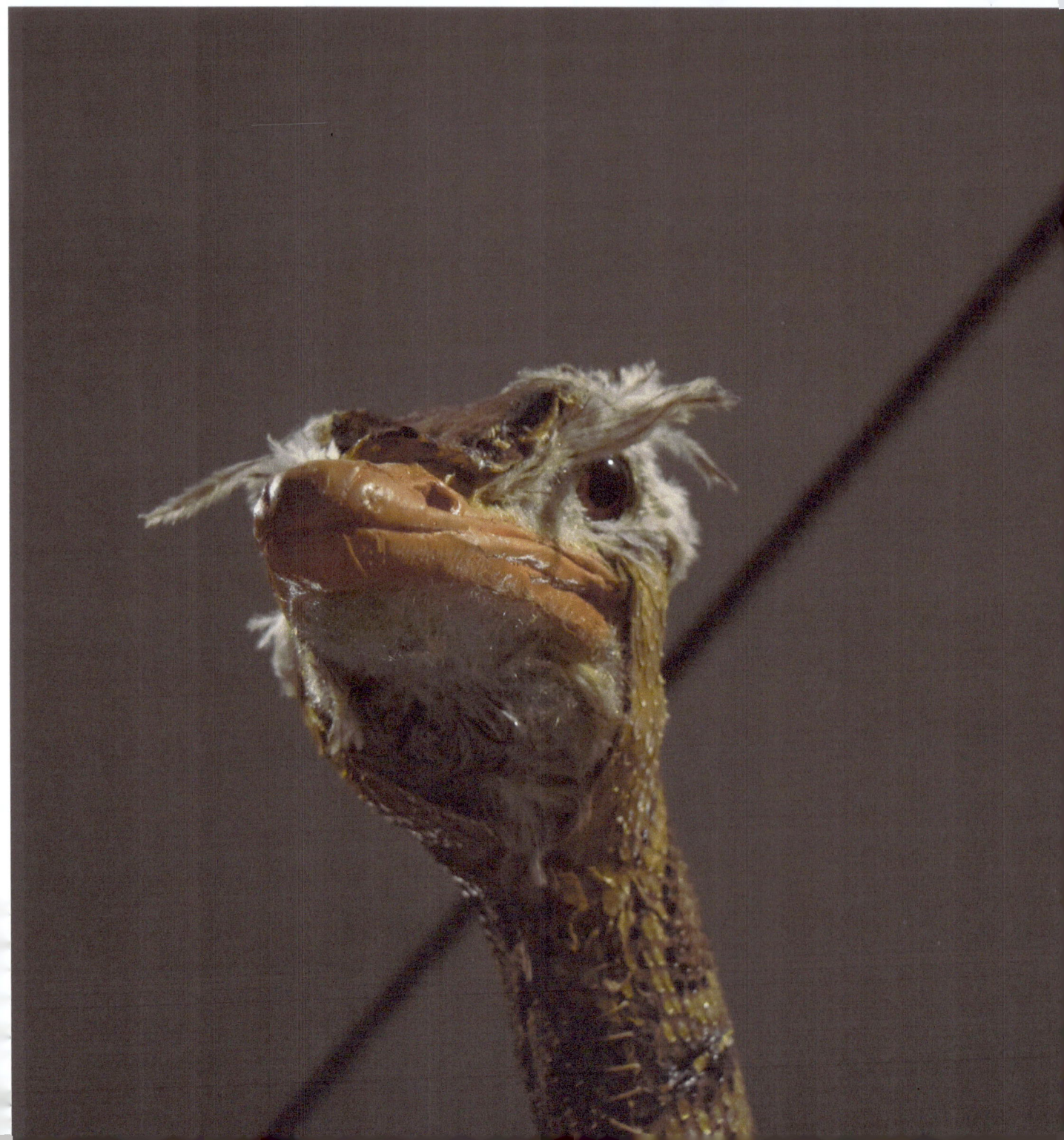

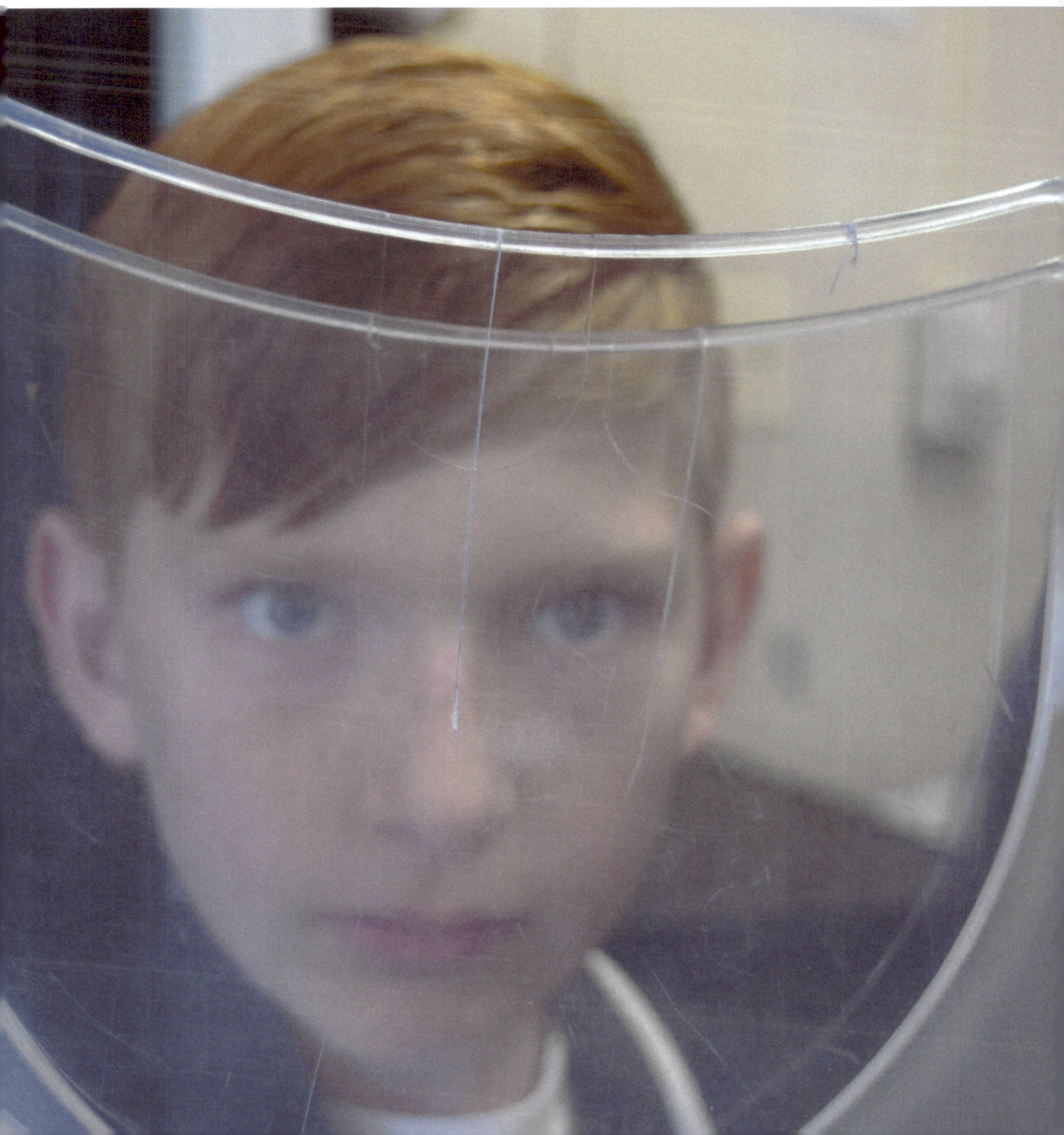

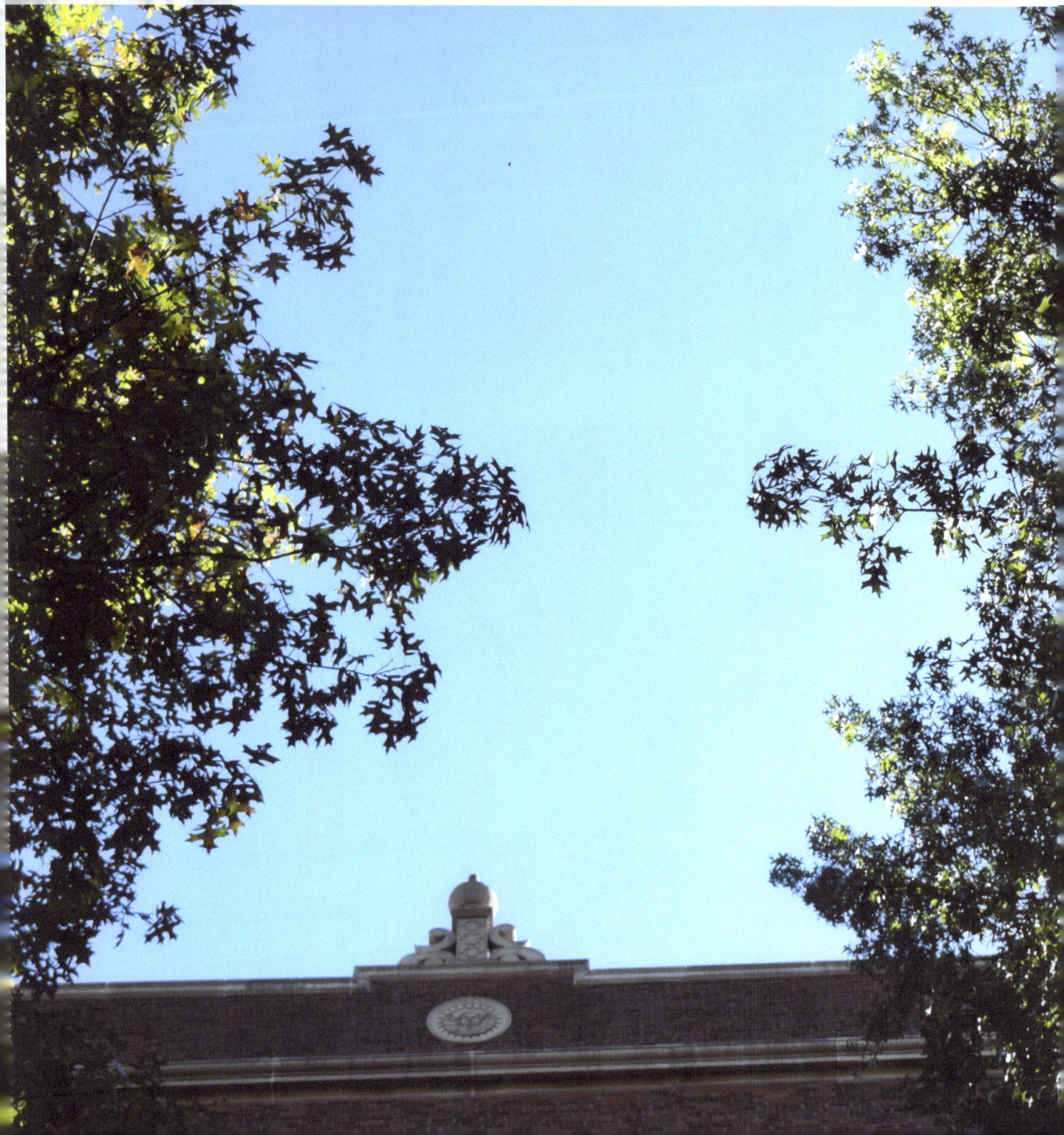

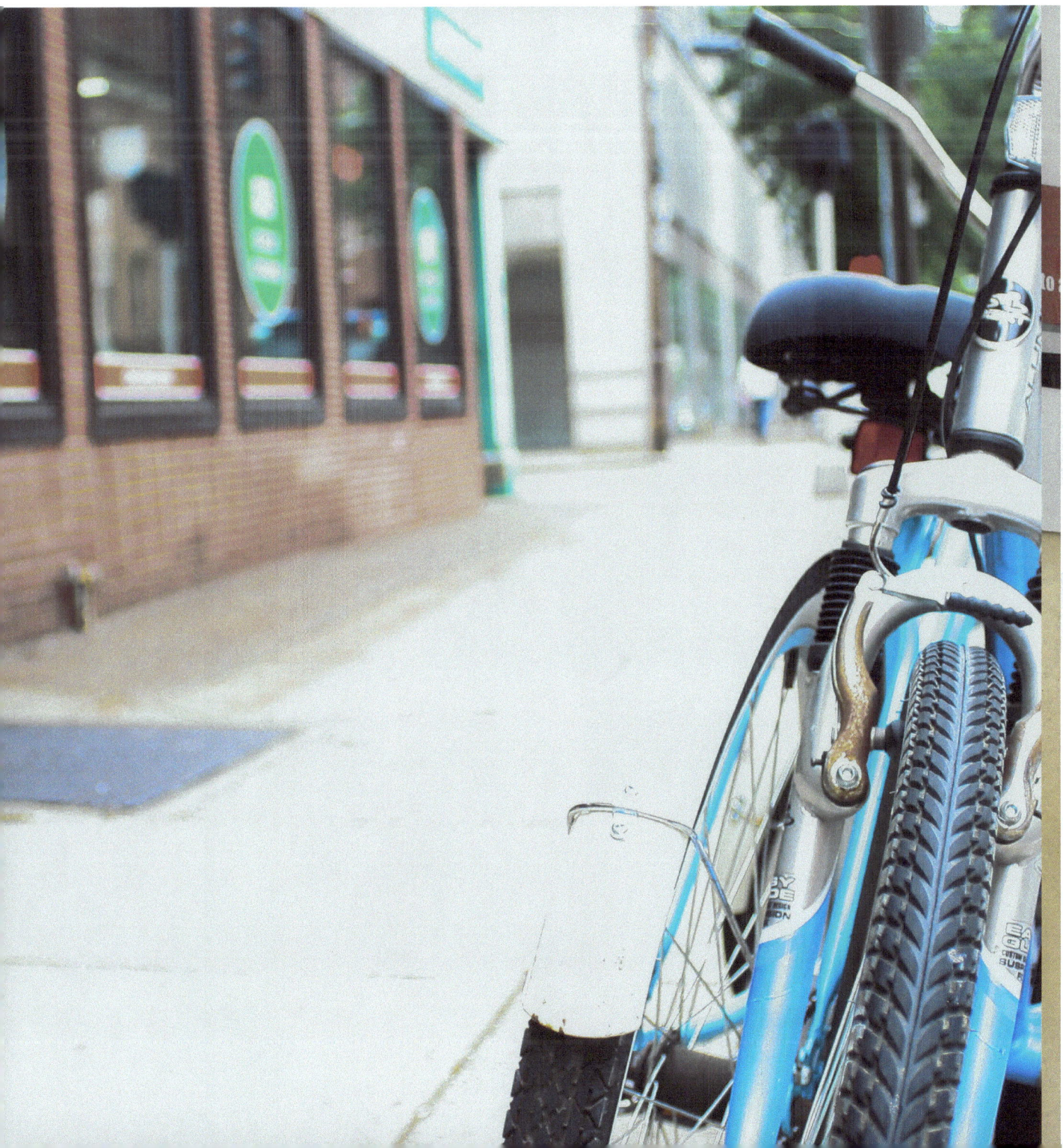

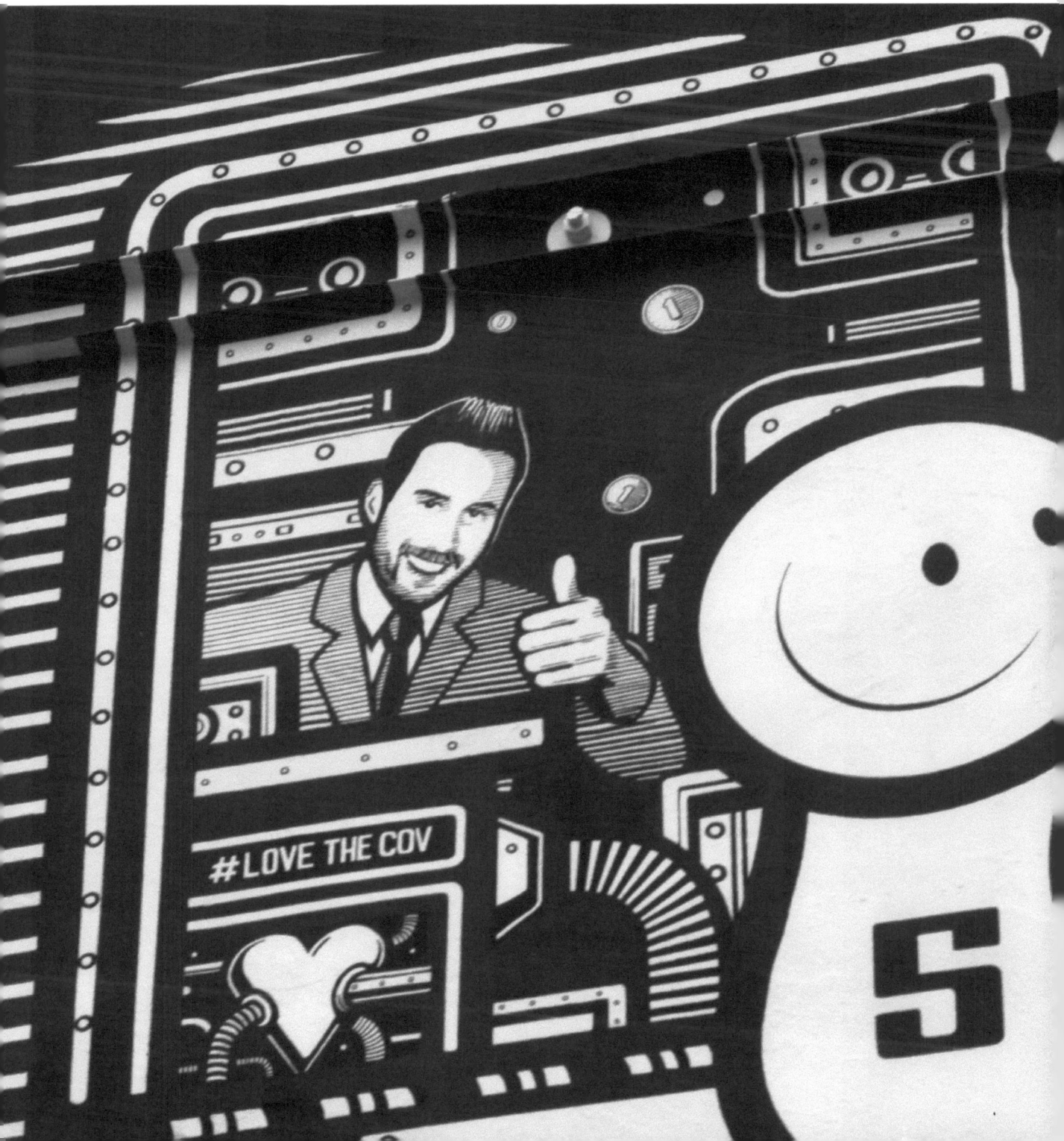

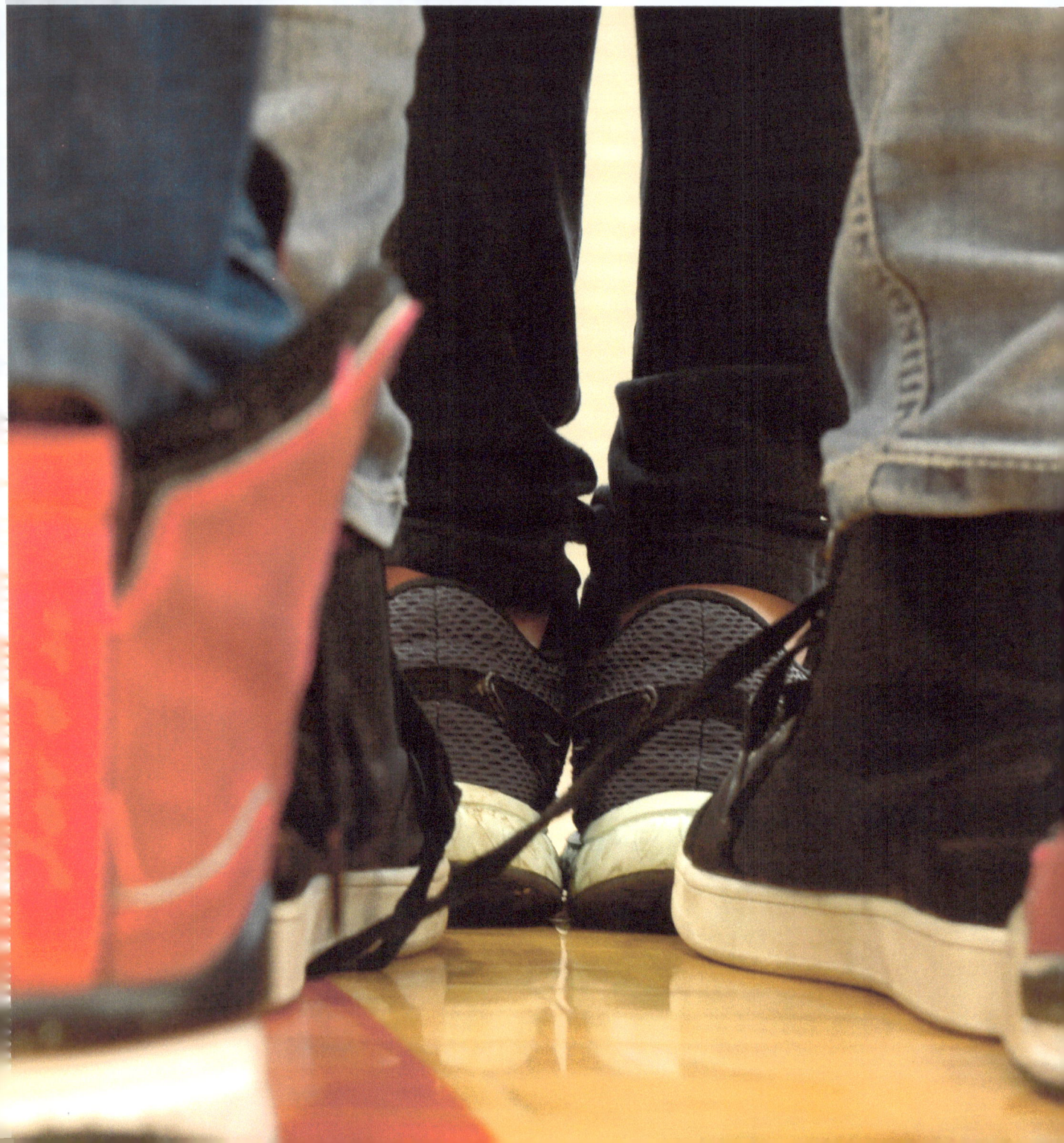

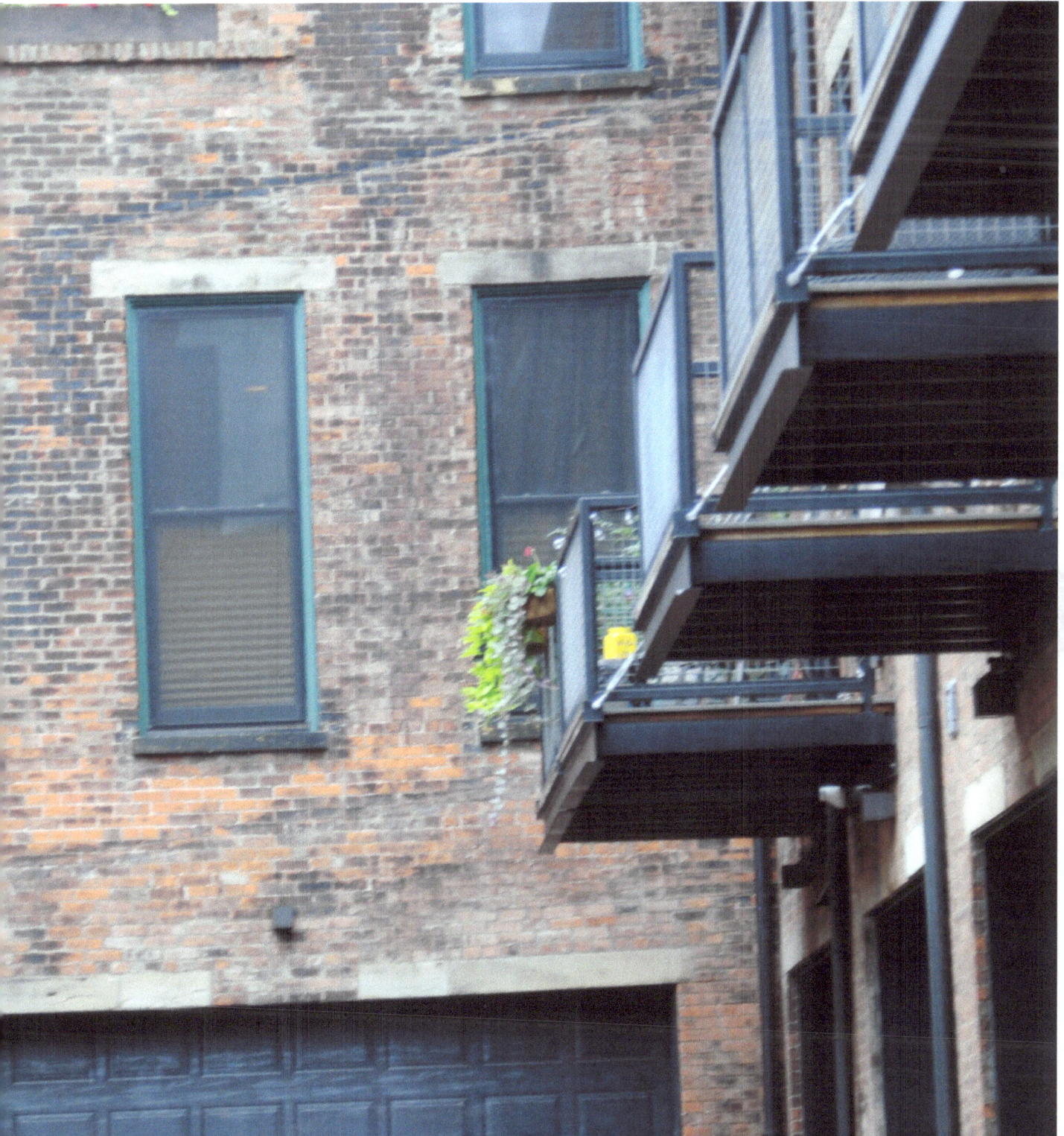

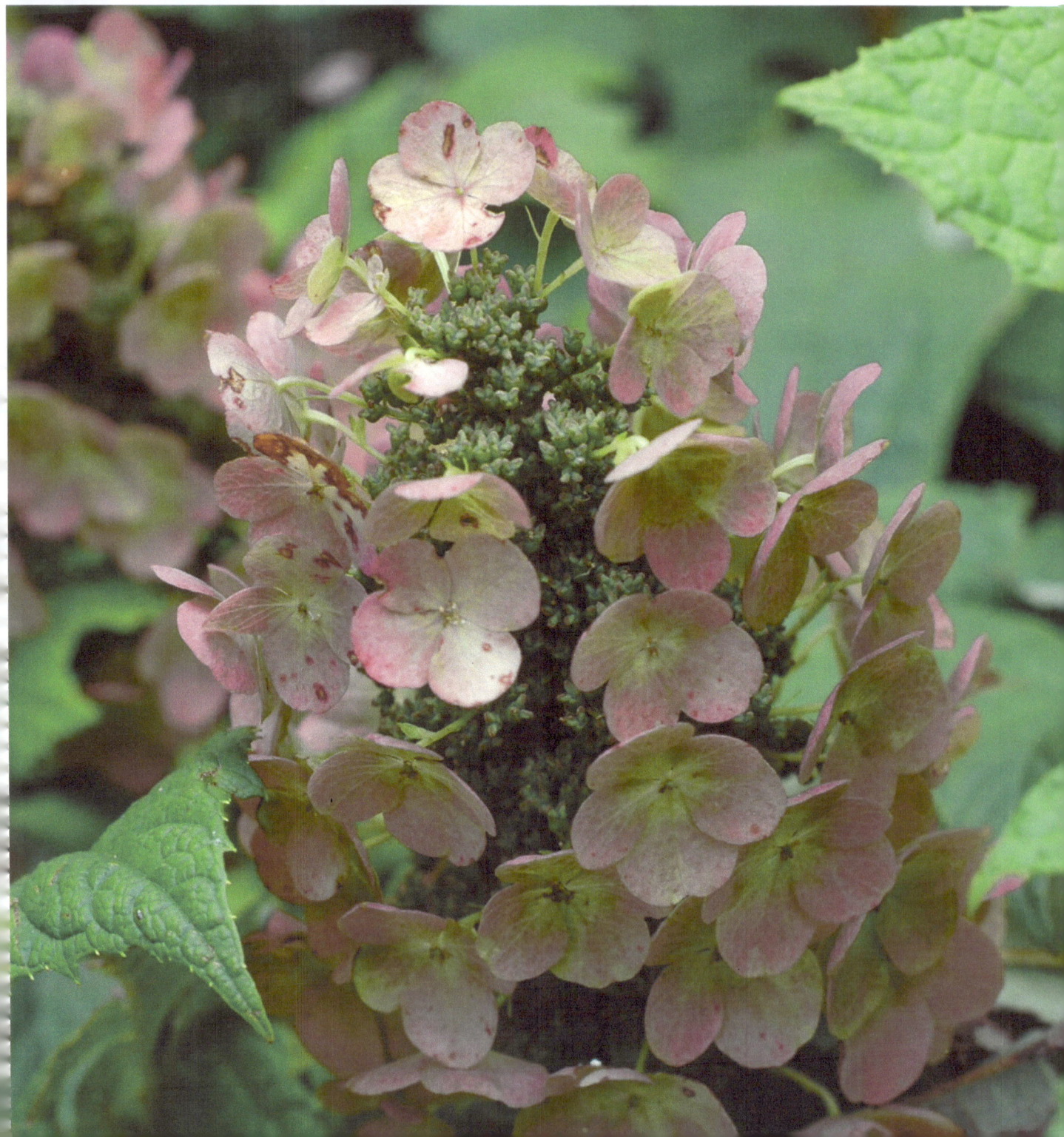

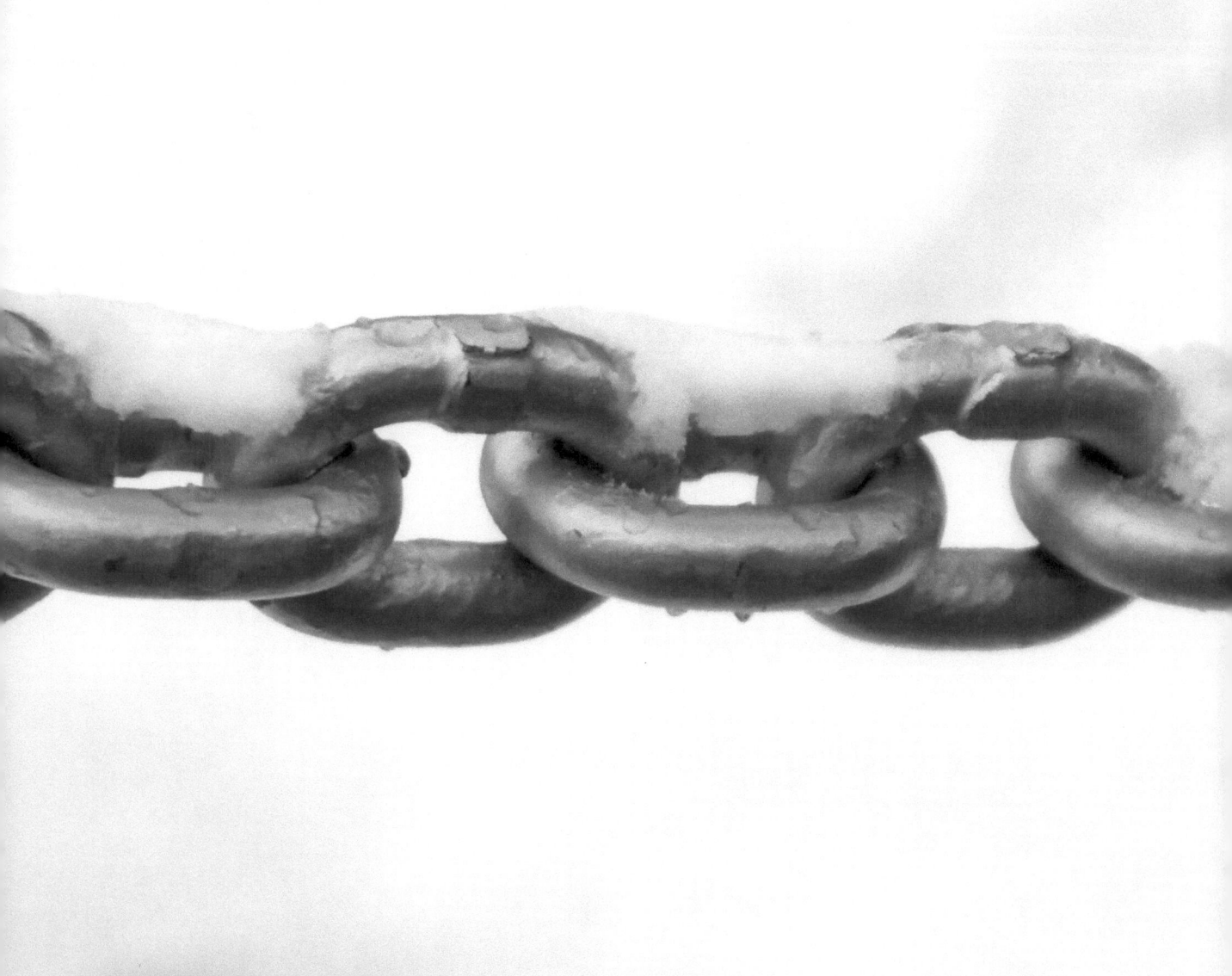

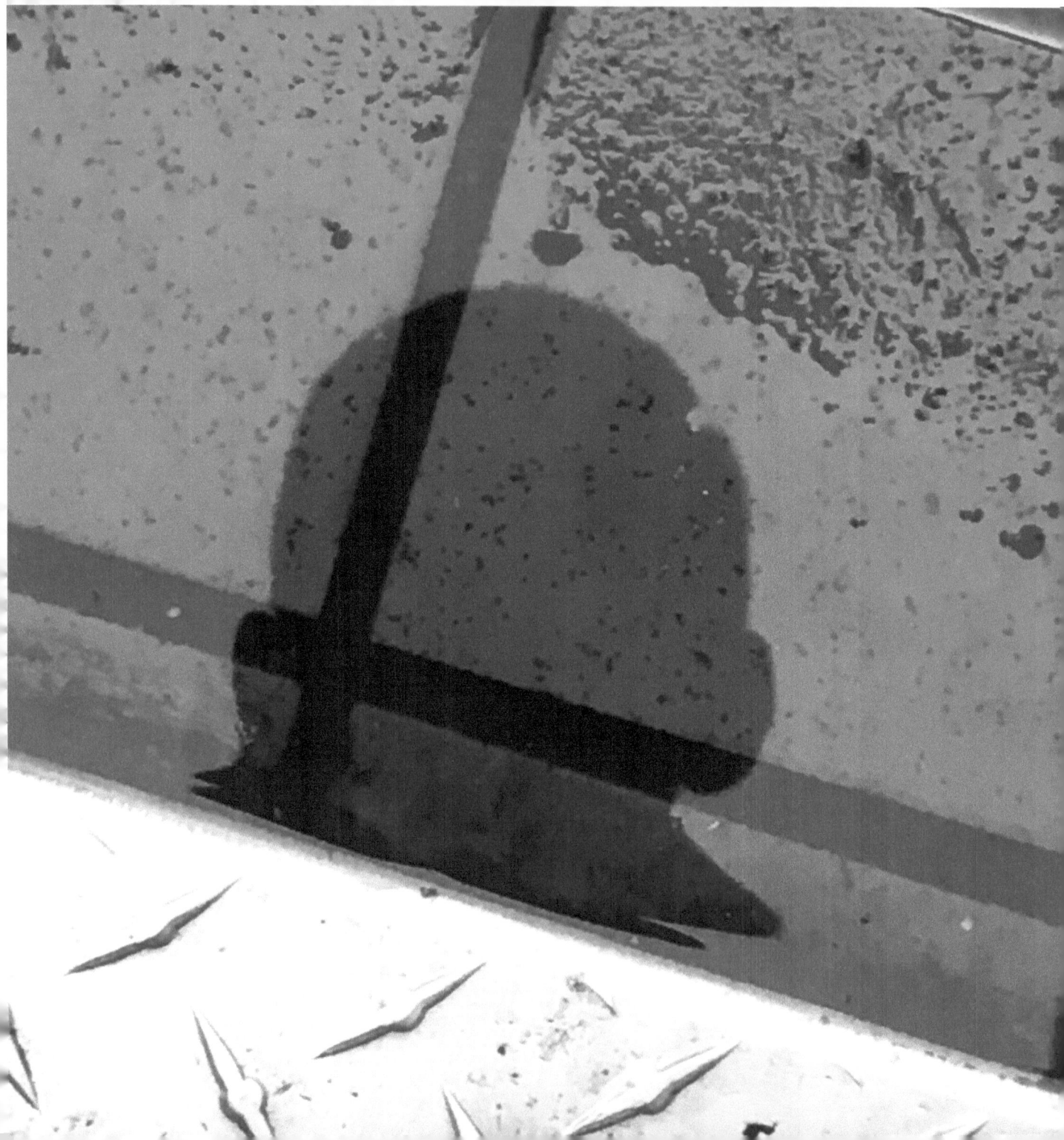

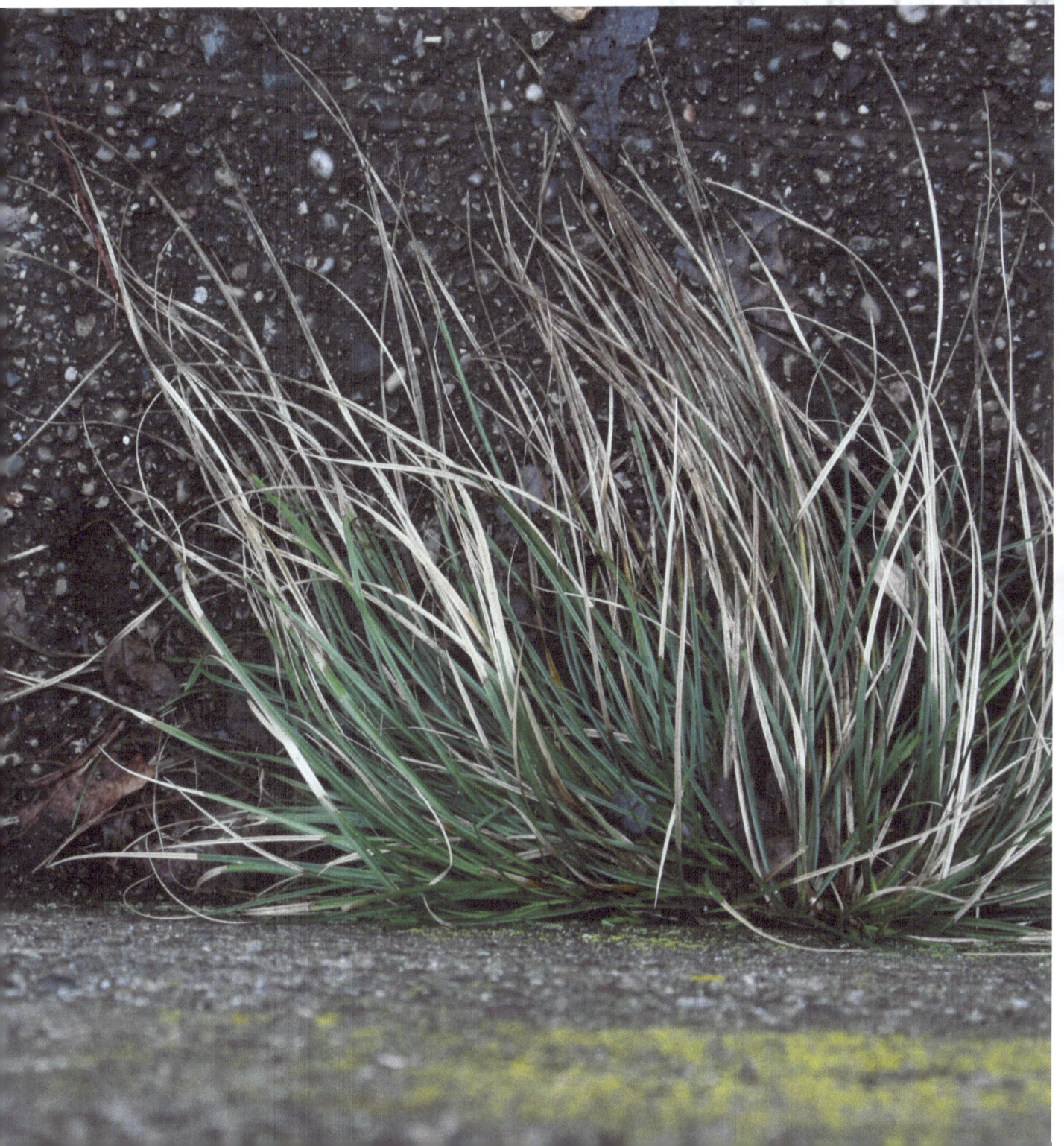

Support i.imagine's non-profit mission

www.iimaginephotography.org

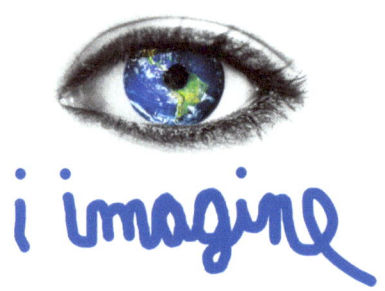

www.ingramcontent.com/pod-product-compliance
Lightning Source LLC
Chambersburg PA
CBHW050726180526
45159CB00003B/1138